Heroic Love
Studies in Sidney and Spenser

HEROIC
LOVE

Studies in Sidney and Spenser

MARK ROSE

Harvard University Press   Cambridge, Massachusetts   1968

© Copyright 1968 by the President and Fellows of Harvard College
All rights reserved
Distributed in Great Britain by Oxford University Press, London
Publication of this book has been aided by a grant from
    the Hyder Edward Rollins Fund
Library of Congress Catalog Card Number 68-29182
Printed in the United States of America

To Phyllis

ACKNOWLEDGMENTS

To Mr. John Buxton of New College, Oxford, I am grateful for his guidance of my first efforts to write on Sidney. An early draft of this book was read by Professors Herschel Baker and Walter Kaiser of Harvard, both of whom were generous with their time and wisdom. To Mr. Baker in particular, as much for his example as for his frequent help over the past years, I owe a debt that I am proud to acknowledge.

The *Arcadia* and *The Faerie Queene* have received considerable attention of late, and the work done has proved informative and stimulating. The studies of Walter R. Davis on Sidney and of Thomas P. Roche, Jr., on Spenser have been especially valuable to me, and I hasten to point out that I am hardly the less indebted to them because I am sometimes prompted to disagree with their conclusions. How much I owe to the writings of the late C. S. Lewis will be obvious. My other debts can only be hinted at or suggested in the notes.

My thanks are due to the following publishers for permission to quote at length from their editions: Cambridge University Press for Albert Feuillerat's *The Prose Works of Sir Philip Sidney;* The Clarendon Press, Oxford, for William Ringler's *The Poems of Sir Philip Sidney;* and The Johns Hopkins Press for *The Works of Edmund Spenser: A Variorum Edition.*

M. R.

Madison, Connecticut
April 1968

CONTENTS

Heroic Love
Studies in Sidney and Spenser

INTRODUCTION

Sixteenth-century readers took a broad and inclusive view of what a good epic could be. Homer, Vergil, Xenophon, Heliodorus, Achilles Tatius, Ariosto, Tasso—each of these men was usually regarded as the author of "an absolute heroic poem," and in this list the Elizabethans proudly included their own Sidney and Spenser.

Sir Philip Sidney's purpose in the *Arcadia,* as has been frequently noted, was identical with Edmund Spenser's in *The Faerie Queene:* the general end of each was "to fashion a gentleman or noble person in vertuous and gentle discipline." [1] A didactic theory of poetry was affirmed by nearly every writer of the Renaissance. Sixteenth-century ideas of the purpose of poetry usually consisted of a combination of Aristotle's conception of imitation and the Horatian dictum that the best poet will simultaneously teach and delight. Not "ryming and versing" make the true poet, says Sidney; rather, "it is that faining notable images of vertues, vices, or what els, with that delightfull teaching, which must be the right describing note to know a Poet by." [2] In their epics, Sidney and Spenser sought to feign notable images that would inspire their gentle readers to the admiration and emulation of virtue. The office of the epic poet was in their conception one of high

---

[1] Spenser, "A Letter of the Authors," *The Works of Edmund Spenser: A Variorum Edition,* ed. Edwin Greenlaw et al., 9 vols. (Baltimore: Johns Hopkins Press, 1932–1949), I, 167. All quotations of Spenser are from this edition, hereafter cited as *Var.* Quotations of *The Faerie Queene* are identified in parentheses in the text. In the case of early texts, my practice throughout has been to normalize *u, v, i,* and *j.* I have also silently altered a few accidentals, expanding abbreviations and removing unnecessary italics for the sake of readability.

[2] *Defense of Poesie,* in *The Prose Works of Sir Philip Sidney,* ed. Albert Feuillerat, 4 vols. (Cambridge: Cambridge University Press, 1962), III, 10–11. All quotations of Sidney's prose are from this edition, with volume and page references given hereafter in parentheses in the text. Quotations of Sidney's poetry are from *The Poems of Sir Philip Sidney,* ed. William A. Ringler, Jr. (Oxford: Clarendon Press, 1962), hereafter cited as Ringler, with page references given in parentheses in the text.

1

INTRODUCTION

responsibility, for to write an epic was not, as Sidney said of Xenophon, merely to bestow one Cyrus upon the world but "to make many Cyrusses."

To the matter of the classical epic the Renaissance added a new subject, love. Vergil had sung of arms and the man, but Ariosto announces that his song is to be "of Dames, of Knights, of armes, of loves delight." [3] In his "Discourses" Tasso remarks that either the ancients did not truly understand love or for some inexplicable reason they did not wish to describe it in heroes, and in the *Defense of Poesie* Sidney mentions the amorous inclinations of modern poets, noting with mock surprise that "even to the Heroical, Cupid hath ambitiously climed" (III, 30). The Renaissance poets understood that in making their heroes lovers they were doing something novel; yet they rarely felt bound to justify their innovation. After all, Dante had held that love was a subject appropriate to the highest style of poetry, and furthermore it was obvious, as Tasso says, that love is noble and beautiful and therefore a passion suitable to heroes.[4]

Naturally the poet's treatment of love was expected to be as edifying as the other parts of his epic, and it is interesting to find Gabriel Harvey recommending the *Arcadia* as a handbook of virtuous loving. "He that will Loove," says Harvey, "let him learne to loove of him that will teach him to Live, and furnish him with many pithy and effectuall instructions." [5] To treat love didactically in a manner that both a graybeard moralist and an enthusiastic youth would approve required both tact

---

[3] *Orlando furioso*, I.1—trans. Sir John Harington (London, 1591).

[4] For Tasso's opinions on love in the epic, see "Discourses on the Heroic Poem," in Allan H. Gilbert, *Literary Criticism: Plato to Dryden* (New York: American Book Co., 1940), esp. p. 485. Dante's remark is to be found in *De vulgaria eloquentia*, II.iv.8.

[5] "Pierce's Supererogation," in G. Gregory Smith, *Elizabethan Critical Essays* (Oxford: Oxford University Press, 1904), II, 263.

and imagination. The temptation was either to avoid the issue completely, by never questioning the virtue of love, or simply to adopt, as Lyly did in *Euphues*, the narrow-minded position of the graybeards, castigating all women as vicious and all amorous passions as folly. Poets of the minor genres might from time to time yield to one or the other of these temptations but, for any epic poet worth his salt, the problem of how to regard love had to be faced seriously and earnestly, and always with the sobering thought in mind that an epic poet was teaching his audience not only how to love but how to live.

How did Sidney and Spenser face this problem? Were they able to reconcile the claims of passion with those of reason? It is with these questions that this book is concerned. In order to point up the moral issues in Sidney and Spenser, I shall first sketch briefly some of the many contradictory doctrines concerning love that were current in Renaissance England. Naturally the attitude a writer takes toward a subject like the value of human love is to a large extent determined by the general philosophical, religious, and cultural atmosphere of his time. The Elizabethan age was the great period of Italian influence on English literature, and Sidney and Spenser were both among the most important purveyors of things Italian. Yet the general atmosphere of Catholic and frequently mystical Italy, the atmosphere that produced Petrarch, Ficino, Bembo, Castiglione, Ariosto, Tasso, and Bruno, was very different from that of England. One of the interesting things that will, I hope, emerge from this study is the manner in which Italian themes and ideas were transformed by the spirit of Protestant England. In England the heroic lover was celebrated not solely because he was a lover but also because he was a prospective husband. Particularly in Spenser's hands, the theme of heroic love received a new birth as that of heroic marriage.

I
THE
MORALITY
OF
LOVE

AN INCONSISTENT HERITAGE:
ASCETICISM, HUMANISM, AND ROMANTICISM

One reason for the Renaissance fascination with love was that it provided the battleground upon which various tendencies of the age struggled for supremacy. Christian asceticism, classical humanism, and medieval romanticism—each of these traditions had its place in the culture of the Renaissance, and each had its peculiar conception of love. The problem was to effect some kind of resolution between the claims of heaven or reason and those of passion.

From an orthodox Christian point of view, passionate love was a sinful involvement with the world. To live after the flesh, Paul had said, was to be against God. Augustine, Paul's spiritual heir, was fated to struggle with a nature unusually passionate, and, having triumphed over his body, he bequeathed to Christianity a rather vicious portrait of his defeated enemy. Enthusiastic hatred of man's embarrassing carnality led to the early glorification of virginity as an ideal. In 390 Jovinian was excommunicated for suggesting that, in the sight of God, the married state might be no worse than virginity. From the detestation of man's natural functions it was but an easy step to the detestation of womankind, whose very existence seemed a threat to virtue, and Jerome, writing against Jovinian, attempted to refute the heretic's defense of matrimony by portraying the evils of woman. Jerome's treatise proved fertile and spawned a vast library of antifeminist writings, in which the daughter of Eve was the representative of all the wicked temptations of the world. To revile woman became no more than an act of piety.

Medieval antifeminism did not suddenly disappear in the Renaissance. The ancient French *querelle des femmes* enjoyed a vigorous life well into the sixteenth century, and the vituperative sonnets that were part of the Petrarchism of the age display an essentially medieval attitude toward woman. It is true that these sonnets were relatively unpopular in England, but the *querelle* had its English counterpart, and all through the sixteenth and early seventeenth centuries a stream of antifeminist pamphlets issued from the English press, with titles like *The Deceite of Women* (1560?) or *The Araignment of Lewd, Idle, Froward, and Unconstant Women* (1615). Even in the idyllic world of the Renaissance pastoral, one discovers attacks on woman that would have pleased a pious medieval misogynist.[1]

In our excitement over the secular spirit of Renaissance Europe, we sometimes forget that the modern world did not at birth wholly reject the asceticism of the Middle Ages. Petrarch in the *Secretum* convinced himself of the sinfulness of the two great passions of his life, his desire for glory and his love of Laura. Even Sidney, great exemplar of the Renaissance man that he was, had his moments of ascetic contempt for the world:

> *Leave me o Love, which reachest but to dust,*
> *And thou my mind aspire to higher things:*
> *Grow rich in that which never taketh rust:*
> *What ever fades, but fading pleasure brings.*
> (*Ringler, p. 161*)

And what was the moral of the whole *Mirror for Magistrates* tradition if not to be wary of seeking one's heaven on earth?

[1] The point is made by Hallett Smith, *Elizabethan Poetry: A Study in Conventions, Meaning, and Expression* (Cambridge: Harvard University Press, 1964), pp. 57–58. On the vituperative sonnets, see Lu Emily Pearson, *Elizabethan Love Conventions* (Berkeley: University of California Press, 1933), pp. 213–214; on the Elizabethan debate about the status of women, see Louis B. Wright, *Middle-Class Culture in Elizabethan England* (Ithaca: Cornell University Press, 1963), pp. 465–507.

THE MORALITY OF LOVE

Still the predominant mood of the Renaissance was not ascetic, and the principal objection of the Renaissance moralist was not that love was a sinful involvement with the world, but that it was debasing to permit one's reason to become subject to passion. Although it was still possible, as Sidney shows, to reject love in the name of heaven, it was more usual to do so in the name of the dignity of man. Thomas Wyatt, for example, invokes Plato and Seneca rather than God in his sonnet bidding farewell to love's baited hooks.[2]

The humanist ethic of reason and temperance implied a remarkably static conception of the good life, an ideal of uninterrupted quiet and peace. To fall in love, to trade the serene content of virtue for the turbulent misery of passion, was to be a fool. About the mildest statement that could be made by the Renaissance moralist concerning love was that of George Puttenham, who allowed that "there is no frailtie in flesh and bloud so excusable as it." [3] Most writers were more vehement, condemning the love of women for different reasons but with the same enthusiasm as the antifeminists of the Middle Ages. If we listened only to the moralists, we would believe that all lovers were at best doomed to lives of misery and repentance and, at worst, to torment, death, and damnation. If we listened in particular to Robert Burton, we might believe that love is not only responsible for innumerable personal calamities but also for many of the greatest public disasters of history. Love is no "virtuous habit," says Burton, "but a vehement perturbation of the mind, a monster of nature, wit, and art." Passionate love "subverts kingdoms, overthrows cities, towns, families; mars,

[2] *Collected Poems*, ed. Kenneth Muir (Cambridge: Harvard University Press, 1950), p. 14.
[3] *The Arte of English Poesie*, ed. Gladys Doidge Willcock and Alice Walker (Cambridge: Cambridge University Press, 1936), p. 48.

9

corrupts, and makes a massacre of men; thunder and lightning, wars, fires, plagues, have not done that mischief to mankind, as this burning lust, this brutish passion." [4]

Ethics, as readers of Burton know, was virtually indistinguishable from medicine, and the second objection of the Elizabethan moralist would be that passionate love is a dangerous physical disorder. The ancient conception that love is a disease was universally accepted in the period, and both the symptoms and the pathology of love were well known to educated men. The most common symptoms—drawn by physicians from those impeccable authorities, Sappho and Ovid—were said to be weeping, sighing, pallor, sleeplessness, alternate seizures of heat and cold, desire for solitude, and loss of appetite. Love was said to begin with an emanation of spirits that passed from the eyes of the lady into the eyes of the lover. Having entered the body, the spirits proceeded to the liver (the seat of the vegetable soul and the humors) and thence to the heart (the seat of the animal soul and the appetite), which they caused to open and emit blood and vital spirit. The excess of blood and spirit produced the first or sanguine stage of the disease, in which the lover felt as if he were burning. This was the less dangerous stage, but if the lady now failed to satisfy her lover's desire, his intense mental activity would consume the excessive heat and he would pass from the sanguine into the melancholy stage, weeping, sighing, and shivering with cold. The prognosis in extreme cases was bad, for the lover was likely to go out of his mind or even die. We recall that Polonius attributes Hamlet's melancholy to love, telling Gertrude and Claudius how he advised Ophelia to disregard the prince's attentions.

[4] *The Anatomy of Melancholy*, III.ii.1.2—ed. A. R. Shilleto (London, 1896), III, 54.

THE MORALITY OF LOVE

And he repelled, a short tale to make,
Fell into a sadness, then into a fast,
Thence to a watch, thence into a weakness,
Thence to a lightness, and, by this declension,
Into the madness wherein now he raves
And all we mourn for.[5]

Dangerous as it might be, love melancholy was still the most glamorous of maladies, and to be in love was the sign of an aristocratic and superior mind. Many a young man—we need think only of Romeo —seems to have been anxious to gain esteem by aping a passion he did not feel, going about, like the "Amorist" in Overbury, "untrust and unbuttoned, ungartred, not out of carelesnes, but care." [6] Stern moralists might criticize Astrophel's passion for Stella, but Thomas Nashe invites the reader of Sidney's sonnets to join in "the admiration of his melancholy." [7]

The glamor of love melancholy was in part the result of a curious semantic confusion. Early Latin translators of Greek manuscripts connected the Greek word *eros* with the Latin words *herus* and *heros,* and consequently believed that their authors meant to associate love with heroism and magnanimity. In the Middle Ages love melancholy was commonly called the malady of "hereos," which in the Renaissance became "heroical love," a disorder obviously appropriate to an epic hero.

---

[5] II.ii.145–150. All quotations of Shakespeare are from *Complete Works,* ed. Peter Alexander (London and Glasgow: Collins, 1951).

[6] *The Overburian Characters to Which Is Added A Wife,* ed. W. J. Paylor (Oxford: Blackwell, 1936), p. 10.

[7] "Preface to *Astrophel and Stella,*" in Smith, *Critical Essays,* II, 224. For full discussion of the lover's disease, see Lawrence Babb, *The Elizabethan Malady: A Study of Melancholia in English Literature from 1580 to 1642* (East Lansing: Michigan State College Press, 1951), esp. chaps. 6 and 8.

Burton explains that it is given this name "because commonly Gallants, Noblemen, and the most generous spirits are possessed with it." [8]

Naturally the esteem in which love was held, the attitude that led poets to believe it a passion appropriate to an epic hero, did not derive exclusively from a semantic confusion. From the time of the troubadours, first among Western poets to express a romantic attitude toward love, much prestige had attached to the passion, so that to be in love became itself proof of nobility. *Cortezia*, according to the troubadours, derived from love, and in medieval France the ability to love was an important distinction between *cortois* and *vilain*. By the sixteenth century, love had become the chief social preoccupation of the Italian upper classes, and numerous "academies" appeared in which gentlemen and ladies met to discuss amorous questions. In Castiglione's *Courtier*, one notes, the question debated is not whether love is an essential part of the gentleman's experience—that is assumed—but only in what way the gentleman should love.[9]

Although conceiving love as an exclusive pleasure, the courtly romantics were in one respect remarkably democratic: only a gentleman could love, but it was true that Cupid could turn even the meanest wretch into a gentleman. "Behold again," says one troubadour poet, "the good things which love gives: it makes a vile creature into a dis-

[8] *Anatomy*, III.ii.1.1 (Shilleto, III, 43). On the semantic confusion behind "heroical love," see J. L. Lowes, "The Loveres Maladye of Hereos," *Modern Philology*, XI (1914), 491–546.

[9] Cf. David Lloyd Stevenson, *The Love-Game Comedy* (New York: Columbia University Press, 1946), p. 113. For points relating to the prestige of love, see Alexander J. Denomy, "Courtly Love and Courtliness," *Speculum*, XXVIII (1953), 44–63; Stanley Leman Galpin, *Cortois and Vilain* (New Haven: Ryder, 1905), pp. 58–66; and Thomas Frederick Crane, *Italian Social Customs of the Sixteenth Century and Their Influence on the Literatures of Europe* (New Haven: Yale University Press, 1920).

tinguished man, a fool into a man of agreeable conversation, a miser into a spendthrift, and it transforms a rascal into a man of honor. By it insane men become sages, the gauche become polished and the haughty are changed into gentle and humble men." [10] Boccaccio included in the *Decameron* the tale of Cymon, in which an uncouth and hopeless fool is transformed by love into a gentleman, a philosopher, a musician, and a knight, becoming the most accomplished young man in Cyprus. And even Iago has heard that "base men being in love have then a nobility in their natures more than is native to them."

The Elizabethans, of course, had their skeptics as well as their moralists and romantics. Shakespeare's Rosalind is one. When Orlando, in true romantic fashion, proclaims he will die if rejected, Rosalind replies with a witty survey of famous lovers, proving that, contrary to romantic opinion, their deaths had nothing to do with love: "Men have died from time to time, and worms have eaten them, but not for love." But skepticism of this sort was relatively rare in the sixteenth century—it was to become more fashionable in the seventeenth—and when the Elizabethans spoke about love, they generally adopted an appropriately solemn tone, either attacking it in the humanist fashion or defending it in the romantic vein. Spenser's defense of love in *The Faerie Queene* is typical:

> *Such ones ill judge of love, that cannot love,*
> *Ne in their frosen hearts feele kindly flame:*
> *For thy they ought not thing unknowne reprove,*
> *Ne naturall affection faultlesse blame,*
> *For fault of few that have abusd the same.*

[10] Aimeric de Pégulhan, quoted in Sidney Painter, *French Chivalry: Chivalric Ideas and Practices in Mediaeval France* (Baltimore: Johns Hopkins Press, 1940), p. 113.

For it of honor and all vertue is
The roote, and brings forth glorious flowres of fame,
That crowne true lovers with immortall blis,
The meed of them that love, and do not live amisse.
(IV.pref.2)

The insistent romanticism of the Elizabethan poets is especially remarkable when we remember that the most popular classical poet at this time was Ovid, hardly a romantic with respect to love. But the Elizabethans, both humanists and romantics, made of Ovid what they wished. The humanists, inheriting the medieval tradition of allegorizing Ovid, assured themselves of his grave morality. Thus Arthur Golding, the earnest translator of Calvin and de Mornay, could believe that his version of the *Metamorphoses* had been a worthy project:

For this doo lerned persons deeme, of Ovids present woorke:
That in no one of all his bookes the which he wrate, doo lurke
Mo darke and secret misteries, mo counselles wise and sage,
Mo good ensamples, mo reprooves of vice in youth and age,
Mo fine inventions too delight, mo matters clerkly knit,
No nor more straunge varietie too shew a lerned wit.[11]

The romantics, too, adapted Ovid to their way of thinking. Marlowe's *Hero and Leander*, libertine, racy, and comic, probably comes closer to

[11] *Shakespeare's Ovid: Being Arthur Golding's Translation of the Metamorphoses*, ed. W. H. D. Rouse (London: Centaur Press, 1961), p. 18. On the popularity of Ovid and the way he was understood in the sixteenth century, see Clyde Barnes Cooper, *Some Elizabethan Opinions of the Poetry and Character of Ovid* (Menasha, Wisc.: George Banta, 1914), and Douglas Bush, *Mythology and the Renaissance Tradition in English Poetry*, rev. ed. (New York: Norton, 1963), esp. pp. 69–73.

the true Ovidian spirit than almost any other work of the century; and yet even Marlowe's poem is as shot through with idealism as it is with libertinism. Leander displays "loves holy fire, with words, with sighs and teares." And he woos in a most unclassical manner:

> *although I am but base,*
> *Base in respect of thee, divine and pure,*
> *Dutifull service may thy love procure,*
> *And I in dutie will excell all other,*
> *As thou in beautie doest exceed loves mother.*[12]

Hero and Leander is unfinished and we cannot know what moral position Marlowe would finally have taken, but it is unlikely that it would have been libertine. There is a certain amount of libertinism or naturalism in the sixteenth century—much early Donne, for example—and libertinism had, from the time of Jean de Meun, a distinguished medieval tradition. But in England this point of view, like skepticism, had to wait until the seventeenth century for its day. Certainly Chapman's conclusion to *Hero and Leander* shuns libertinism and, for that matter, romanticism as well. Chapman explains that lovers' delights require judgment. And his judgment is severe: "Love is a golden bubble full of dreames, / That waking breakes, and fils us with extreames." [13]

---

[12] I.193, 218–222—*Works,* ed. C. F. Tucker Brooke (Oxford: Oxford University Press, 1910), p. 497.

[13] III.9, 231–232 (Brooke, pp. 515, 520). On libertinism, see Louis I. Bredvold, "The Naturalism of Donne in Relation to Some Renaissance Traditions," *Journal of English and Germanic Philology,* XXII (1923), 471–502; Aldo D. Scaglione, *Nature and Love in the Late Middle Ages* (Berkeley: University of California Press, 1963); and Bush, *Mythology and the Renaissance Tradition,* p. 133, who provides a useful collection of references to libertine arguments in Elizabethan literature.

HEROIC LOVE

Neither skepticism nor libertinism, then, was in serious competition with the romanticism of the age. The real threat to the romantics was from the humanists, the sage moralists who might, like Chapman, come along to prove that all their fine ideas were but a golden bubble.

The romantic view of love reached Chaucer and his contemporaries through the literature of medieval France, but the principal source for the romanticism of the Renaissance was the literature of Italy. The passion celebrated by the troubadours and their successors in northern France was, beneath its courtly garb, ordinary physical desire. However, the poets of the *dolce stil nuovo*—Cavalcanti, Dante, and the other early Italians—were too high-minded to celebrate so mundane a love. In their verse the passion described became less the desire for physical possession of one beautiful lady than the greater desire for possession of the eternal idea of beauty. The lady herself was elevated to the status of a transcendent being, an intelligence or angel, a manifestation of the ultimate divinity. To love this divine lady was, finally, to love God, and now the passion of the lover was ennobling because it was spiritually illuminating.

What the *stilnovisti* sought was a synthesis of the conflicting attitudes toward love and, in particular, a reconciliation of Christian teaching with troubadour romanticism. Their quest suggests the essential difference between the medieval and the Renaissance attitude toward love. The Middle Ages seem to have been content to dwell in divided and distinguished worlds by turns, applauding with equal sincerity both the praise of love and the rejection of love. Andreas Capellanus, after two books very much in the service of Cupid, turns about face to denounce love in the third book of *De amore*. Chaucer, after five books of *Troilus and Criseyde*, makes a similar turnabout, advising "yonge, fresshe folkes" to put all mere earthly loves aside and

16

THE MORALITY OF LOVE

Repeyreth hom fro worldly vanite,
And of youre herte up casteth the visage
To thilke God that after his image
Yow made, and thinketh al nis but a faire
This world, that passeth soone as floures faire.[14]

The man of the Middle Ages was often hardly aware that his loyalties were divided. The troubadours, for instance, appear to be quite ignorant that, from a Christian point of view, the love they praise is sinful.[15] Even when he perceived that his ideals were in conflict, the medieval writer did not necessarily feel compelled to resolve the issue; sometimes he was willing merely to state the case on each side and let it go at that. The conflict in *The Owl and the Nightingale* is perhaps between representatives of heavenly and earthly love, but the issue is never resolved. At the end of the poem the two birds fly off to Master Nicholas for a judgment of their respective claims, but what that judgment is we never, in true *débat* fashion, learn.

The *stilnovisti*, feeling the claims of both reason and passion, were the first important poets not to be satisfied with this sort of moral schizophrenia, and the resolution they worked out indicates the subsequent direction of Italian love literature. As we shall see, the Renaissance finally arrived at two ways of resolving the conflicting claims: one—the way of Platonic mysticism—was especially characteristic of Italian thought; the other, based upon a new attitude toward matri-

[14] V. 1837–1841–*Works*, ed. F. N. Robinson (Boston: Houghton Mifflin, 1957), p. 479.
[15] See Alexander J. Denomy, *"Fin' Amors:* The Pure Love of the Troubadours, Its Amorality, and Possible Source," *Mediaeval Studies*, VII (1945), 179–183. For an excellent survey of the development of romantic ideas on love from the troubadours through the *stilnovisti*, see Maurice Valency, *In Praise of Love: An Introduction to the Love-Poetry of the Renaissance* (New York: Macmillan, 1958).

17

mony, was particularly congenial to the Protestant and relatively commonsensical mind of England.

RATIONALIZING PASSION: NEOPLATONISM AND ROMANTIC MARRIAGE

The great love poet of Italy is Petrarch and with him, rather than the *stilnovisti*, the Renaissance proper begins. Petrarch's works illustrate all the conflicting philosophies of love with which the Renaissance had to struggle, from the ascetic rejection of earthly love that appears from time to time in the *Canzoniere* and that triumphs in the *Secretum*, to the romantic approbation of "Benedetto sia 'l giorno" or the humanist rejection of uncontrolled passion in "Voglia mi sprona." The conception of love in the *Canzoniere* is hardly simple. The sequence is less a consistent praise of love than a *battaglia d'amore*, a confused struggle of contradictory desires that leaves the poet in the moral chaos typified by "S'amor non è," the famous sonnet in which Petrarch confesses that he has no idea whether love is good or bad or even whether he loves according to his own will: so confused, so tormented, is he that he can do nothing but complain.

While his mistress lives, the poet can find no peace but, like Dante's Beatrice, Laura dies and a quasi-mystical resolution follows. Not being the thoroughgoing mystic that Dante was, Petrarch never wholly identifies his lady with the divine principle; yet since he now finds his passion directed perforce toward heaven, he believes that love for Laura will lead to salvation, to the blissful day when, freed from mortal darkness, his soul will soar into the "bel sereno" and he will see his lady and his God. Clearly in the tradition of the *stilnovisti*, Petrarch's resolution is not, strictly speaking, Platonic, but it is suggestive of the

18

general tendency in Italy toward a mystical and Platonic resolution. It was a simple matter for the Neoplatonists of the later Renaissance to reinterpret Petrarch in the light of their philosophy and to claim him as one of the great teachers of true love, and in fact the Neoplatonists quote from Petrarch more often than from Plato himself.

Renaissance Neoplatonism becomes a definite movement in the middle of the fifteenth century, with the founding of the Platonic Academy in Florence under Ficino. Ficino's Latin *Commentary on Plato's Symposium* was published in 1496, providing the model for a new literary genre, the *trattato d'amore*, which proliferated in the sixteenth century and greatly influenced the ideas of the time. The Neoplatonists produced a number of other serious works, most notably the treatises of Leone Ebreo and Giordano Bruno, but these difficult, abstruse books were not of the kind to have a broad appeal. It was Bembo's *Asolani* and Castiglione's *Cortegiano* that, together, exerted the widest direct influence in the sixteenth century. Both works derive ultimately from Ficino, but in them the interest is as much literary as philosophical, and the philosophy is considerably diluted.[1]

The essential doctrine of Neoplatonism is the ladder of love, the notion that, earthly beauty being a shadow of divine beauty, the lover ascends from worship of the world to worship of God. For Ficino, as for Plato, the bottom rung of the ladder was masculine beauty, but Bembo soon made the crucial change, substituting the beauty of woman.

[1] On the love treatises and Neoplatonism generally, see John Charles Nelson, *Renaissance Theory of Love: The Context of Giordano Bruno's Eroici Furori* (New York: Columbia University Press, 1958); Crane, *Italian Social Customs,* esp. chaps. 3 and 4; and Nesca A. Robb, *Neoplatonism of the Italian Renaissance* (London: Allen and Unwin, 1953). Useful points are also to be found in John Smith Harrison, *Platonism in English Poetry of the Sixteenth and Seventeenth Centuries* (New York: Columbia University Press, 1903). The standard discussion of Ficino is Paul Oskar Kristeller, *The Philosophy of Marsilio Ficino,* trans. Virginia Conant (New York: Columbia University Press, 1943).

Renaissance Neoplatonism had a double nature. If a writer emphasized love's divine end, he was actually proposing something very like the ascetic ideal of the Middle Ages, and many in fact regarded the sexual side of love with contempt, admitting the necessity of sexual intercourse only with the reluctance of a Paul. But if the writer chose to emphasize the mundane means to the divine end, he might use Neoplatonic ideas to rationalize and dignify a very earthly passion.

Bembo's *Asolani* reveals how self-consciously the Renaissance writer sought through Neoplatonism to resolve his moral confusion. *Gli Asolani* is divided into three sections, each presenting a different attitude toward love: first Perottino's denunciation of love's evils, then Gismondo's praise of love's virtues, and finally Lavinello's exposition of Neoplatonic philosophy. The treatise thus progresses by thesis and antithesis, with Neoplatonism providing the crowning synthesis, a unified ethic of love.

Neoplatonism, however, never provided a completely satisfactory resolution. Among other things, there always remained the problem of how to square its concept of virtuous passion with the humanist ethic of right reason. Count Lewis raises this problem in the fourth book of *The Courtier* when he prods Bembo to his great speech, saying, "the opinion of many is, that it is unpossible for love to stand with reason." [2] Bembo's famous speech attempts to describe a reasonable love. Actually the ecstatic love he envisions is at least as passionate as any other form of love: what Castiglione really presents is the paradox of a reasonable passion, a paradox somewhat obscured by the brilliant rhetoric of the speech. Giordano Bruno, a much more careful philosopher than Castiglione, treated the same problem more subtly, if less eloquently. Having adopted an Aristotelian definition of virtue as the mean between two

[2] *The Book of the Courtier,* trans. Sir Thomas Hoby, ed. Walter Raleigh (London: Nutt, 1900), p. 352.

extremes, Bruno concedes that the Neoplatonic passion is a vice; yet he insists that it is a noble vice. The true love frenzy, he says, "differs from other more ignoble frenzies not as virtue differs from vice, but as vice practised in a divine way by a more divine subject differs from vice practised in a bestial way by a more bestial subject." Any frenzy is an evil but, since this particular passion leads us to an ultimate good, it is not an absolute evil. This is the closest Bruno comes to calling love good. The claims of right reason were so fundamental and so strongly felt that, no matter how pure the passion he was advocating, he could not avoid some equivocation.[3]

A second problem with the Neoplatonic solution was credibility. Not even the authors themselves—the authors of the more popular treatises, at any rate—really believe their philosophy to be practical. In Ficino, the lover who can rise from earthly to heavenly beauty belongs to an elite, but he is not beyond the pale of normal humanity, for every man desires the same good. In Bembo, however, the Neoplatonic lover is a saint, a hermit wholly divorced from ordinary mankind and its desires. And in Castiglione, the Neoplatonic ecstasy is reserved for the aged, since "the nature of man in youthfull age is so much inclined to sense, it may be graunted the Courtier, while he is yong, to love sensuallye." [4] Apparently a trivial afterthought, this concession to youthful desires in fact reduces Neoplatonism from a serious ethic to little more than an elegant subject for polite discussion.

Ficino and his followers distinguished between three kinds of passion: divine love, which raises man to heights of spiritual contemplation; human love, a vague middle state marked by limited sensual pleasure; and bestial love or unlimited voluptuousness. With the

---

[3] *The Heroic Frenzies,* trans. Paul Eugene Memmo, Jr. (Chapel Hill: University of North Carolina Press, 1965), pp. 100, 111.
[4] *Courtier,* p. 352.

elimination of divine love as a practical possibility, the majority would find themselves in the middle condition of human love and, morally, this condition was ambiguous. "Granted," says Bembo's hermit, "that it is not evil like those which are mingled with bestial desires; still it falls short of virtue because it does not draw you toward an immortal object but holds you midway between the extremes of desire where it is not safe to remain, for on a slope it is easier to slide into the depths than to clamber to the summit." [5] Still, dangerous as it might be, this middle love was better than nothing, for from it a man might some day ascend to the higher passion.

Ultimately, then, Neoplatonism failed to provide a resolution. Human love was still a phenomenon of uncertain moral status. Passionate love had been only imperfectly reconciled with the dictates of right reason. But the lover had been provided with a new set of arguments with which to defend his passion. He might now claim that his love was of the spirit as much as the body and was therefore a noble passion. And he might claim the added dignity of a relationship, however distant, between his ardor and the ecstasy of the celestial vision.

The Neoplatonism of the Italian Renaissance arrived in England together with Petrarchism. Many gentlemen read such authors as Bembo and Castiglione in the original, and, for those without a command of Italian, there were numerous translations, among them Hoby's version of The Courtier. By the final decades of the sixteenth century, fashionable literature in England, especially the sonnet sequences, epyllia, and court dramas, resounded with echoes of Italian Neoplatonism.

Although Neoplatonism is important in Elizabethan literature, its significance has often been exaggerated. Excepting two or three poems,

[5] Gli Asolani, trans. Rudolf B. Gottfried (Bloomington: Indiana University Press, 1954), p. 186.

almost nothing written in sixteenth-century England demonstrates much interest in the more serious Neoplatonists. The great Ficino, so popular on the Continent, was almost unknown in Elizabethan England. In Britain Neoplatonism was little more than a literary fad for a few poetic ideas and for certain turns of expression, derived not from Ficino but from sources at several removes, the Italian popularizers and the French Petrarchists. Even the scope of this fad has been exaggerated. Sidney's "Leave me o Love," for example, is frequently cited as a specimen of Elizabethan Neoplatonism when in fact it is an expression of Christian *contemptus mundi,* containing little that would have been alien to Chaucer.[6] The most thoroughgoing Neoplatonist of the Elizabethan period is usually said to be the eclectic Edmund Spenser, but Robert Ellrodt in his comprehensive study of the subject finds little in Spenser that can be called specifically Neoplatonic, outside a few sonnets in the *Amoretti* and the *Fowre Hymnes.* Spenser emerges from Ellrodt's discussion as a practical moralist with little taste for esoteric speculation. Perhaps even the *Hymnes* owe less to Neoplatonic thought than is sometimes imagined. As C. S. Lewis some time ago suggested, these poems "are substantially meditations on chivalrous, monogamous, English love, enriched with colourings from Plato, Ficino, Lucretius, and the medieval poets. If we speak of the Platonic colourings at all we have to do so at some length because they are difficult: not because they are of immense importance."[7]

[6] Harrison, for example, takes it as an illustration of "the appeal which Platonism made to the English poets in its doctrine of a heavenly love" (*Platonism in English Poetry,* p. 85), and see also Smith, *Elizabethan Poetry,* p. 26. In "Ficino and the Platonism of the English Rennaissance," *Comparative Literature,* IV (1952), 214–238, Sears Jayne discusses how little the Elizabethans were interested in the serious Neoplatonists.

[7] *English Literature in the Sixteenth Century* (Oxford: Oxford University Press, 1954), p. 376. For Ellrodt's views, see *Neoplatonism in the Poetry of Spenser* (Geneva: E. Droz, 1960).

HEROIC LOVE

Amatory literature in sixteenth-century England is, in general, more down to earth and practical, less mystical and Neoplatonic, than the Italian models on which it is based. Broadly speaking, the English sonneteers are more sensual, less elevated, than the Italians. Many critics have emphasized the derivative nature of Elizabethan sonnets, but it is interesting to note that, no matter how closely the Elizabethans imitate Petrarch and his school, not one English sequence follows the master's model in having the lady die and the lover's passion continue for her in heaven. In the genre of the courtesy book, too, there is a great difference between the English and the Italian productions. The Italian works frequently treat love idealistically and mystically, as in Castiglione; the English courtesy books are by comparison homely and prosaic, and love, when treated at all, is generally regarded from a purely practical point of view. The duties and responsibilities of marriage rather than the ecstasies of idealistic love are the usual subjects of the English courtesy books.[8]

Nowhere does the characteristic domesticity of the Elizabethans emerge more distinctly than in those works which show the influence of the Italian love treatises. Edmund Tilney's *Flower of Friendshippe*, for example, is a set of dialogues in the Italian manner which owes much both to Castiglione and to the "questions" episode of Boccaccio's *Filocolo*. In *The Flower of Friendshippe* the narrator and a friend,

---

[8] The point about English sequences not following the Italian pattern is made by Lisle Cecil John, *The Elizabethan Sonnet Sequences: Studies in Conventional Conceits* (New York: Columbia University Press, 1938), pp. 172–173. On the English courtesy books, see Ruth Kelso, *The Doctrine of the English Gentleman in the Sixteenth Century* (Urbana: University of Illinois Press, 1929), esp. p. 85, and John E. Mason, *Gentlefolk in the Making: Studies in the History of English Courtesy Literature and Related Topics from 1531 to 1774* (Philadelphia: University of Pennsylvania Press, 1935), esp. pp. 15, 32, and 35. I am not of course including *The Faerie Queene* in this category, even though it might be considered a courtesy book of sorts.

walking out on a spring day, come to a noblewoman's house where they find a company of ladies and gentlemen, including Vives and Erasmus, assembled for dinner. The newcomers join the group for the afternoon's entertainment, which is to be discussion of a set topic, marital love, a subject chosen as appropriate for spring, the season of "naturall amitie." How is amity maintained in marriage? Through the partners' knowledge of their duties. Accordingly, Tilney's philosophers proceed to delineate the duties of the married man, reconvening the following afternoon to consider those of the married woman. Together, the two days' discussions form a complete marriage manual, a practical guide to the good life as Tilney understands it. Men are counseled to avoid gaming and rioting, to provide well for their households, to avoid jealousy, and to be careful about educating their children. Women are advised to be obedient, to avoid excess in apparel, to pass over their husbands' defects, to keep their houses in order, and to take care with meat dishes, for it is "a great want in a woman, if she be unskilfull in dressing of meate." [9] As in Bembo, then, the set topic is one of love and, as in Castiglione, it concerns the formulation of an ideal figure. But the love that interests Tilney is married affection rather than extramarital passion, and the ideal figure is not the graceful courtier but that very domestic creature, the perfect husband or wife.

Elizabethan domesticity also prevails in George Whetstone's *Heptameron of Civill Discourses*. This book, a collection of brief tales set in a general dramatic frame of polite dialogues about love, takes its title from the *Decameron* and the French *Heptaméron* but is actually modeled on *The Courtier*. Castiglione's mysticism, however, was lost

---

[9] Edition of 1568, sig. E4ᵛ. On Tilney's sources, see Crane, *Italian Social Customs*, p. 511. Crane regards all three of the writers I cite, Whetstone and Greene as well as Tilney, as representative examples of the Elizabethan use of Italian materials.

25

upon his English imitator. As in Tilney, the subject is domestic life and married love, with a defense of matrimony, a very long consideration of how to make a happy union, and many "Householde Lawes, to keepe the Maried, in Love, Peace, and Amitie." [10]

Neither *The Flower of Friendshippe* nor the *Heptameron* is particularly Neoplatonic in atmosphere; yet even when the English do absorb some of the philosophical coloring of their models, they do not necessarily treat love in quite the Neoplatonic manner. One section of Robert Greene's *Morando: The Tritameron of Love* consists of a debate on whether it is good to love and is cast in a tripartite form that clearly recalls Bembo's *Asolani*. First Sostrata presents love's evils, then Sylvestro its virtues, and finally Panthia expounds a third point of view that synthesizes the earlier attitudes. Panthia's speech, corresponding to Lavinello's exposition of Neoplatonism in *Gli Asolani*, is overlaid with vaguely Neoplatonic distinctions between love of spirit and love of body, but stripped to essentials her position is that a passion leading to marriage is virtuous while one existing for the moment alone is a vice. Nowhere does she reveal even perfunctory interest in the crucial concept of the ladder of love.[11]

The practical domesticity of the English may have something to do with that vague concept, national character; it also has a good deal to do with the more tangible fact that England was Protestant. In the minds of the Protestant reformers, marriage acquired a dignity almost unknown in previous Christian thought. The reformers denied matrimony

[10] Edition of 1582, sig. X4ᵛ. On Whetstone's relationship to Castiglione, see Crane, pp. 520–521, n. 5, and Thomas C. Izard, *George Whetstone: Mid-Elizabethan Gentleman of Letters* (New York: Columbia University Press, 1942), p. 114.

[11] For Panthia's speech, see the edition of 1584, sig. E4ᵛ, and on *Morando's* Italian sources, John Clark Jordan, *Robert Greene* (New York: Columbia University Press, 1915), pp. 20–22.

the status of a sacrament, but, equally important, they assaulted the ancient ascetic ideal of the Catholic Church. Virtually unchallenged, the orthodox tradition of Paul, Jerome, and Augustine, exalting virginity at the expense of marriage, had dominated the Middle Ages in England as well as throughout the rest of Christendom. John Wyclif, it is true, advocated marriage for the clergy in order to put down lechery, but Wyclif never attacked asceticism itself. On the contrary, he asserted upon the authority of "Seint Austin and Jerom" that, though "matrimonie be good and gretly comendid of God," still "clene virginite is moche betre." [12] The sixteenth-century reformers went further and challenged the ideal as well as the practice of the Church, and, so far as England was concerned, the ascetic ideal was largely defeated.

At first the attacks came from humanists within the Church, men like Erasmus, as well as from reformers without—but the most vehement assaults were delivered by the Protestants. The folly of the Catholics' exaltation of virginity is a persistent theme in Calvin. He blames them for "a superstitious admiration of celibacy" and "extravagant encomiums on virginity," the result of which was that, "though marriage was not condemned as impure, yet its dignity was so diminished, and its sanctity obscured, that he who did not refrain from it was not considered as aspiring to perfection with sufficient fortitude of mind." Calvin acknowledges that virginity is holy, but he conceives of marriage as a calling equally holy, "for those who are denied the gift of continence, are undoubtedly called to marriage by the voice of God." [13]

[12] "Of Weddid Men and Wifis," *Select English Works,* ed. Thomas Arnold (Oxford, 1869–1871), III, 190.

[13] *Institutes of the Christian Religion,* IV.xii.27, xiii.17—trans. John Allen (Philadelphia: Presbyterian Board of Christian Education, 1936), II, 527, 549. Seeking as he did the restoration of the thought and practices of the primitive church, Calvin managed to convince himself that even Paul was a supporter of marriage. See *Institutes,* IV.xii.24.

27

HEROIC LOVE

The moral status of matrimony was one of the great issues of the later Renaissance. Whereas the Council of Trent declared anathema all who denied the superiority of celibacy, the Protestants were dwelling more and more upon the virtues of marriage until matrimony seemed not merely equal but in many ways superior to virginity. Thus William Perkins says that "mariage of it selfe is a thing indifferent, and the kingdom of God stands no more in it, then in meates and drinkes; and yet it is a state in itselfe, farre more excellent, then the condition of single life." Or, to take an example from popular literature, Greene's Panthia says that "though Diana hath reapt renowne by her chastity, yet Juno hath gained more honour by her Mariage." The result of this novel attitude was a flood of really extravagant encomiums on marriage, as exemplified by this seventeenth-century specimen taken from Daniel Rogers' *Matrimoniall Honour:*

Marriage is the Preservative of Chastity, the Seminary of the Commonwealth, the seed-plot of the Church, pillar (under God) of the world, right-hand of providence, supporter of lawes, states, orders, offices, gifts and services: the glory of peace, the sinewes of warre, the maintenance of policy, the life of the dead, the solace of the living, the ambition of virginity, the foundation of Countries, Cities, Universities, succession of Families, Crownes, and Kingdomes; Yea (besides the being of these) its the welbeing of them being made, and whatsoever is excellent in them, or any other thing, the very furniture of heaven (in a kinde) depending thereupon.

What had happened was that in Protestant England matrimony had gradually become not merely a praiseworthy state, but a duty, a virtue, and almost a kind of religious order. "Our Maker bids increase," Milton was to write, "who bids abstain / But our Destroyer, foe to God and Man?" [14]

As the Protestant understanding of matrimony matured, social changes were taking place that would also contribute to Elizabethan attitudes. The status of women in the Middle Ages was not high; their freedom was severely limited, and their education neglected. But in the sixteenth century, partially as a result of the new dignifying of marriage, their prestige and freedom greatly increased. That a woman sat upon the throne influenced opinions of the sex, and great ladies throughout the land took Elizabeth as their model. Female education first became a concern in the Tudor period, and some ladies of the time were very learned indeed—the daughters of Sir Thomas More, Lady Jane Grey, and Elizabeth herself being only some of the more familiar examples. William Harrison remarks that besides having "sound knowledge of the Greeke and Latine toongs," many gentlewomen are "no lesse skilfull in the Spanish, Italian, and French," and adds that in these studies English women "come verye little or nothing at all behind" their husbands.[15] The contrast with the ladies of the Middle

[14] Perkins, *Workes* (London, 1612–1613), III, 671; Greene, *Morando*, sig. E4ʳ; Rogers, quoted in William and Malleville Haller, "The Puritan Art of Love," *Huntington Library Quarterly*, V (1942), 246–247; Milton, *Paradise Lost*, IV.748–749—ed. Helen Darbishire (Oxford: Oxford University Press, 1952). For fuller discussion of English attitudes toward matrimony, see, besides the Hallers' seminal essay, Charles and Katherine George, *The Protestant Mind of the English Reformation* (Princeton: Princeton University Press, 1961), pp. 257–305.

[15] "The Description of England," *Holinshed's Chronicles* (London, 1807), I, 330. On the new position of women, see Chilton Latham Powell, *English Domestic Relations, 1487–1653: A Study of Matrimony and Family Life in Theory and Practice* (New York: Columbia University Press, 1917), and Foster Watson, *Vives and the Renascence Education of Women* (New York: Longmans, Green, 1912), pp. 1–28. Mason deals briefly with the education of women in *Gentlefolk in the Making*, pp. 54–57.

Ages is sharp. The most significant female devotee of learning in England before the Renaissance seems to have been Margaret, Countess of Richmond and Derby, the mother of Henry VII and founder of Christ's and St. John's Colleges, Cambridge. Yet Margaret knew only enough Latin for the saying of service; her greatest skill was in needlework.

There is also a contrast between the ladies of England and their counterparts in the Catholic countries. Although Catholic women, too, enjoyed new dignity, their freedom of action does not seem to have equaled that of the English. Thus Italian travelers were puzzled by the readiness of English ladies to accept dinner invitations from foreign gentlemen. Spanish travelers were not merely puzzled but scandalized, and during Mary's reign many Spanish gentlewomen refused to attend court because of the English ladies' free conversation. There was a popular saying on the Continent: "England is a paradise for women, a prison for servants, and a hell for horses." [16]

Matrimony's new status, combined with the novel role of women, led in England to a romanticizing of marriage, to a fusion, perhaps, of the medieval idealization of love and the Protestant attitude toward wedlock. This is not to say that marital affection had never been regarded in a romantic light before the sixteenth century; on the contrary, scholars have at times exaggerated the extent to which the idealized passion of the Middle Ages was necessarily adulterous. Chrétien de Troyes did indeed write the *Lancelot*, but he also composed the *Yvain*, in which the hero, having offended his wife, devotes himself to aiding distressed damsels to prove his worth to his lady and spouse. A romantic conception of marriage is apparent in Chaucer's *Franklin's*

[16] For these points, see Lewis Einstein, *The Italian Renaissance in England* (New York: Columbia University Press, 1913), pp. 223–224; the same writer's *Tudor Ideals* (New York: Harcourt, Brace, 1921), p. 127; and Powell, *English Domestic Relations*, pp. 174–175.

Tale, and this attitude may even, if we accept Kittredge's interpretation, be identified as Chaucer's own. In the Middle Ages, however, married love was not the dominant theme: from the troubadours to *Troilus and Criseyde,* most of the energies of medieval poets went into celebration of adulterous love, and, in Italy, the passions of Dante, Petrarch, and the Neoplatonists had nothing to do with marriage. [17]

The flourishing of the romantic attitude led to a changed emphasis in the whole conception of matrimony. Traditionally, the three objects of Christian marriage were, in order of importance, procreation, relief of concupiscence, and consolation of loneliness. Protestants increasingly dwelt upon the last of these objects—the meet and happy conversation between the partners, as Milton put it—with the result that they began to conceive of marriage more as a concord of love than a physical or economic union. By the end of the sixteenth century, even a conservative like Hooker believed love to be "the perfectest ground of wedlock." Indeed, so much moral significance attached to love that a man's affection for his wife was often interpreted as evidence of godliness and virtue. Sir John Harington, who in his youth wrote an encomium on marriage, provides a good example of this point of view. "I am of the Censor Cato his mind," he says in one of the chatty notes in his Ariosto, "who being a marvelous austere man otherwise, yet pronounced flatly that a man could not be an honest man, that was not to his wife a kinde man. And I will go thus much farther, that you shall hardly

[17] That a fusion of the medieval idealization of love and the Protestant attitude toward matrimony did indeed occur is, in somewhat different terms, the general thesis of C. S. Lewis' *Allegory of Love* (Oxford: Oxford University Press, 1936). By listing adultery as one of the "four marks" of courtly love (p. 12), Lewis gives the impression that the romantic passion of the Middle Ages was always adulterous. Much the same impression is given by Alexander J. Denomy, *The Heresy of Courtly Love* (New York: McMullen, 1947), esp. pp. 22–23. For Kittredge's interpretation of "Chaucer's Discussion of Marriage," see *Modern Philology,* IX (1912), 435–467.

find a discreet loving husband . . . but is withall a vertuous good minded man." Harington's faith in affectionate husbands is a position that can be carried to extremes, as it is by Master Pedro, Tilney's spokesman in *The Flower of Friendshippe*, who solemnly cites as an example of a virtuous husband "our father Adam," the first to die for love of his wife.[18]

In the traditional view, matrimony was too consequential to allow for the preferences of the young people. Children were to put themselves entirely in the experienced hands of their parents. According to Vives, who wrote a popular treatise on the subject, young ladies should even refrain from showing an interest in wedlock, since "it is not comely for a maide to desire mariage, and muche lesse to shew hir selfe to longe therfore." And as for chancing to become enamoured of her intended, Vives warns that "if shee love him afore she have him . . . what shal he thinke but that she will as lightly love an other as shee hath doone him, whome as yet shee oughte to shewe no love unto." Vives' book was read throughout the sixteenth century, and arranged marriages were probably still the norm among all classes in England. By the end of the century, however, frequent protests indicate that old-fashioned opinions were losing favor. One of Whetstone's characters argues that the partners of an arranged union will "turne to flat fowle falling out," their household will disintegrate, and their friends and relatives will be put at odds; but free choice for young people will

---

[18] Hooker, *Of the Laws of Ecclesiastical Polity*, V.lxxiii.2—*Works*, ed. John Keble (Oxford, 1845), II, 427; Harington, edition of 1591, sig. D3ʳ; Tilney, sig. B4ʳ. On the new emphasis in the Protestant conception of matrimony, see Haller, "Puritan Art of Love," pp. 235–272. In "Hail Wedded Love," *ELH*, XIII (1946), 79–97, William Haller discusses Milton's liberal views on divorce as a logical development of this new emphasis. If true matrimony was a marriage of minds, then, in Milton's opinion, a union without spiritual accord was no union at all.

produce "as much love betweene the Married, as the other sowed debate." And according to an early seventeenth-century guide to matrimony, free choice no longer requires defense: "the voice of the world speakes for it, and accounts that match much more miserable then death itselfe, in which love is not used as the match-maker, yea, and the match-keeper, to." [19]

Romantics that they were, the Elizabethans had by no means thrown caution entirely to the winds. Except in extraordinary circumstances, a young man was still expected to obtain his father's approval before marrying. The disguised Polixenes asks Florizel in *The Winter's Tale* whether his father is not mad or senile if the youth is marrying without his knowledge.

> *Reason my son*
> *Should choose himself a wife; but as good reason*
> *The father—all whose joy is nothing else*
> *But fair posterity—should hold some counsel*
> *In such a business.*　　　　*(IV.iv.398–402)*

The Elizabethans, no matter how highly they rated love, still predicted sad futures for those who married without parental consent. Harington

---

[19] Vives, *The Instruction of a Christen Woman,* trans. Richard Hyrde (London, 1557), sigs. P2^r, Q3^r–Q3^v. Hyrde's translation, first published around 1529, went through eight editions by 1592. Whetstone, *Heptameron,* sigs. F2^r, I1^r. The *Heptameron* devotes the second and third days' discussions to arranged marriages. William Whately, *A Bride-Bush* (London, 1619), sigs. B6^r–B6^v. On arranged marriages in England, see Einstein, *Tudor Ideals,* pp. 245–251; Powell, *English Domestic Relations,* pp. 14–15; and George Elliott Howard, *A History of Matrimonial Institutions Chiefly in England and the United States* (Chicago: University of Chicago Press, 1904), I, 399–403. The subject also figures in Kenneth Thorpe Rowe, *Romantic Love and Parental Authority in Sydney's Arcadia,* University of Michigan Contributions in Modern Philology, No. 4 (Ann Arbor, 1947).

warns young ladies that even though they choose most worthy men, "yet if it be without their parents good will, it seldome prospers, but is full of diverse misadventures and hazards, that many times be the cause of their utter ruine." [20] The ideal was the coinciding of parental reason and youthful passion. Then the Englishman supposed he had achieved what the Neoplatonist in a different way had achieved, a reasonable passion.

By idealizing marriage, then, Protestant England found a resolution for some of the conflicting ideas about love, but one that depended upon the happy coincidence of youthful and parental wishes. What if the two failed to coincide? The resulting conflict between love and duty was to prove remarkably fruitful as a literary subject. Being essentially insoluble, it was to be exploited again and again, especially by writers for the stage, where, from Shakespeare's time to the present, it has been a staple commodity. The theme might be used for comedy by fashioning the plot around a magical denouement, as in *A Midsummer Night's Dream,* or it might be used for tragedy, as in *Romeo and Juliet.*

Like the Neoplatonic resolution, that of Elizabethan England really consisted of the approval of passionate love not for its own sake but because it could be transformed into something finer: married love. As we shall see, the Protestant resolution actually involved a paradox. Marriage was now a supreme goal, but to reach this goal one first had to yield to passionate love—and this, from the point of view of humanist ethics, was still morally suspect.

[20] *Orlando furioso,* sig. I4^r.

II
THE
ARCADIA

LOVE IN THE TWO ARCADIAS

The Countesse of Pembrokes Arcadia draws upon a number of traditions for material: the Greek romances, the romances of chivalry, and the Renaissance pastoral romances.[1] Perhaps the most interesting thing to be learned from a study of these traditions is the extent to which the Englishman has moralized his sources. There are of course two *Arcadias*, Sidney's original version, the *Old Arcadia* as it is called, which was probably completed in 1580, and the monumental revision, the *New Arcadia*, on which Sidney was still working when he died. Yet even before he decided to transform his relatively slight romance into an epic, Sidney seems to have conceived his purpose as didactic, for the *Old Arcadia* is suffused with a moral earnestness notably absent from its sources. In the Greek romances, for example, the assumption that fortune rules everything and that man is without free will produces stories that are exciting in their sequences of unpredictable events; morally, however, these romances are frivolous. The *Arcadia*, so closely resembling the Greek romances in both its versions, insists at every turn upon the importance of moral choice. The *Old Arcadia*, in fact, opens with an analysis of Basilius' decision to retire into the country to avoid fulfillment of the prophecy that appears to threaten his family and his state.

In both the *Old* and the *New Arcadia* much of Sidney's attention is focused upon the morality of passionate love. But the attitude toward love in the two versions is not precisely the same. In the *Old Arcadia* greater weight is given to the humanist ethic of reason. Generally speaking, the *Old Arcadia* portrays the transformation of Pyrocles and Musidorus from models of virtue into examples of the follies and dangers of passionate excess; it has relatively little to say about the

[1] Sidney's principal sources include Heliodorus' *Aethiopica*, Achilles Tatius' *Clitophon and Leucippe*, Malory's *Mort D'Arthur*, Book XI of *Amadis de Gaul*, Sannazaro's *Arcadia*, Montemayor's *Diana*, and Gil Polo's *Diana enamorada*.

37

virtues of love. Sidney's disapproval of passion is revealed with a humor and lightness of touch alien to the more severe Elizabethan moralists, but his position is largely similar to theirs, and the *Old Arcadia* is a work that in complexity of moral understanding probably should stand closer to Lyly's *Euphues* than to Spenser's subtle and sophisticated *Faerie Queene*.

The *New Arcadia*, however, is a fit companion for Spenser's epic. In making his original pastoral romance into a heroic poem, one of the things Sidney did was to restore the balance between reason and passion: the *New Arcadia* permits the serious claims of love to be put forward for consideration. In the *Old Arcadia* the princes, once they have become the lovers of Pamela and Philoclea, are treated with constant irony and appear quite ridiculous; in the *New Arcadia* they retain some of their dignity. This change is partially the result of the suppression of the often mocking narrator of the original version; also important are the many alterations in detail which in the *New Arcadia* are designed to increase the reader's respect for Pyrocles and Musidorus.[2] Above all, Sidney's additions to his story establish a context in which the loves of the princes can be viewed in a more favorable light. The Urania episode suggests the nature of an ideal passion. The long captivity episode of Book III, in which Pamela and Philoclea conduct

[2] For a good example of the mocking narrator of the *Old Arcadia*, see Feuillerat, IV, 34. (Volume IV of Feuillerat's edition contains the original *Arcadia*, first printed in 1926). In the *Old Arcadia* Pyrocles' impresa as an Amazon is "an Egle covered with the fethers of a Dove, and yet lying under an other Dove, in suche sorte, as it seemed, the Dove prayed uppon the Egle" (IV, 24). In the revised version, the emblem is changed to a figure of Hercules. Comparison of the princes' first disputation (I, 55–59) with the corresponding passage in the *Old Arcadia* (IV, 10–14) reveals a number of fairly typical minor changes, each of which serves to increase the dignity of the enamoured Pyrocles. On the treatment of love in the two versions, see Neil L. Rudenstine, *Sidney's Poetic Development* (Cambridge: Harvard University Press, 1967), pp. 24–28.

themselves so admirably in the hands of Cecropia, answers the questions of the misogynist about whether women are capable of virtue. The first part of the tale of Argalus and Parthenia, in which the hero remains faithful despite the heroine's mutilation, indicates that even ordinary human love may be something more than lust for physical beauty. The second part of this tale, in which Parthenia seeks death at the hands of her husband's slayer, suggests that in some circumstances love can indeed be the spur to noble deeds. So, too, the story of Queen Helen of Corinth and her desperate love for Amphialus was probably intended, although Sidney never lived to conclude it, to represent another virtuous passion. In Book II Sidney gives Pyrocles a speech that seems to reflect something of his own attitude toward Helen: "You may see by her example (in her selfe wise, and of others beloved) that neither follie is the cause of vehement Love, nor reproch the effect. For never (I thinke) was there any woman, that with more unremoveable determination gave her selfe to the councell of Love, after she had once set before her mind the worthines of your cousin Amphialus, and yet is nether her wisedome doubted of, nor honour blemished" (I, 283–284). Even the episode of Phalantus' tourney leaves the reader more favorably disposed toward the princes, for, by contrasting their ardor with the insincerity of Phalantus and Artesia, it makes genuine passion appear a rare and valuable thing.

Unfortunately, Sidney's revision of his work breaks off in midsentence in Book III, and the text with which we must deal consists of the partial revision to which was added, by the authority of the Countess of Pembroke, a somewhat altered version of the final three books of the *Old Arcadia*. To what extent does this composite *Arcadia* represent the author's intentions? Have we any guarantee that the conclusion of the revised *Arcadia* would even remotely have resembled that of the original version? We have of course no guarantee, and yet it seems likely that the Countess did her brother no disservice in preparing the text she did. The oracle of Apollo with which the *Old Arcadia* opens shows that, at the time he composed this poem, Sidney had his entire plot in mind, and the same oracle is, with only minor changes, used in the *New Arcadia*, suggesting that he meant to conclude his revised story as he had the first. Furthermore, very close to the end of the revised portion, Sidney has inserted a second oracle in which the god advises Basilius that his daughters are about to be released from captivity and commands that the king remain in retirement until both he and Philanax are "fully agreed in the understanding of the former prophecie" (I, 510). In other words, Sidney does not at this late point appear to have changed his mind about how to conclude his story. That this is so need not be surprising, considering his method of revision. In transforming the *Old Arcadia* into the *New*, Sidney discarded hardly a page of his original text. Rather than canceling the first draft and beginning anew, what he has done is to introduce a great deal of fresh incidental narrative. He changed the disposition of his original story and made numerous revisions in detail, but the essential text of the *Old Arcadia* persists, embedded in the midst of the new material. The result is that, although the effect of the story is very different, the central plot of the *New Arcadia* is almost identical with that of the *Old*. There seems no substantial reason to suppose that Sidney would not have continued the revision in this manner.

One significant change in the main story was necessary, however. In Book III of the *Old Arcadia* Pamela elopes with Musidorus who, overcome with physical desire, is only by good fortune saved from breaking his oath to preserve her chastity until they are married. Meanwhile Pyrocles, having contrived to gain access to Philoclea's chamber, does succeed in consummating his desire. These incidents occur in that part of the work which Sidney had not yet reached in his revision;

THE ARCADIA

nevertheless, in the folio authorized by the Countess, they do not appear in their original form. In this text Musidorus merely steals an innocent kiss from the sleeping Pamela, and Pyrocles with equal chastity falls asleep in the arms of his beloved. It used to be thought that these changes represent the Countess' bowdlerization of her brother's lusty work. But recent scholarship has held that the alterations were made either by Sidney himself or upon his authority,[3] and this opinion seems correct to me. The need for the changes was probably clear to Sidney. In the *Old Arcadia*, where the scales were weighted so heavily on the side of reason, these episodes exemplified the kind of vice to which love can lead and were essential to Sidney's moral purpose. But if left to stand in the revised version, they would have undercut the new emphasis on the virtues of love.

Of course I am principally concerned with the revised *Arcadia*, the version which is a heroic poem and in which the attitude toward love is the most interesting. The text of this version is far from satisfactory and therefore must be approached with tact, but the composite text does, I believe, represent Sidney's general intentions.

IDEALISM IN AN IMPERFECT WORLD

It was primarily from Jacopo Sannazaro's *Arcadia* that Sidney derived the ideal landscape of pastoral tradition, the unlocalized land of silver

---

[3] See esp. Kenneth Thorpe Rowe, "Elizabethan Morality and the Folio Revisions of Sidney's *Arcadia*," *Modern Philology*, XXXVII (1939), 151–172; Ringler, pp. 375–378; and William Leigh Godshalk, "Sidney's Revision of the *Arcadia*, Books III–V," *Philological Quarterly*, XLIII (1964), 171–184. See also Joan Rees, "Fulke Greville and the Revisions of *Arcadia*," *Review of English Studies*, XVII (1966), 54–57, who agrees that the revisions are Sidney's own, but suggests that perhaps they were intended for the *Old Arcadia* only and not necessarily for the *New*.

41

streams and enameled meadows. Entering Sidney's country of Arcadia we find ourselves in a familiar place, a traditional dream world of natural peace and harmony far surpassing any earthly reality:

There were hilles which garnished their proud heights with stately trees: humble valleys, whose base estate semed comforted with refreshing of silver rivers: medows, enameld with al sorts of ey-pleasing floures: thickets, which being lined with most pleasant shade, were witnessed so to by the chereful deposition of many wel-tuned birds: each pasture stored with sheep feeding with sober security, while the prety lambs with bleting oratory craved the dams comfort: here a shepheards boy piping, as though he should never be old: there a yong shepherdesse knitting, and withall singing, and it seemed that her voice comforted her hands to work, and her hands kept time to her voices musicke. (I, 13)

But Sidney's Arcadia is more than landscape; he has enlarged the significance of the pastoral ideal by allowing Arcadia to become an authentic country, a recognizable political entity, famous "among all the provinces of Greece . . . for the well tempered minds of the people." Peace and harmony, the essential characteristics of the ideal landscape he inherited, remain the essential characteristics of Sidney's political state. The citizens of Arcadia never indulge in war; they are "not sturred with false praise to trouble others quiet, thinking it a small reward for the wasting of their owne lives in ravening, that their posteritie should long after saye, they had done so." And the internal affairs of Arcadia are as harmonious as its foreign policy is peaceful. The ruler is Basilius, "a Prince of sufficient skill to governe so quiet a countrie, where the good minds of the former princes had set down good lawes, and the well bringing up of the people doth serve as a most sure bond to hold them" (I, 19). Once again we recognize where we are: we have come upon the familiar Elizabethan utopia of the well-ordered monarchy.

The connection between the ideal landscape and the utopian state is for Sidney far from casual. Musidorus passes through Laconia on his way to Arcadia and learns that this barren, wasted land has been reduced to its present condition "by a civill warre, which being these two yeares within the bowels of that estate, betweene the gentlemen and the peasants (by them named Helots) hath in this sorte as it were disfigured the face of nature, and made it so unhospitall as now you have found it." Arcadia is flourishing precisely because it is domestically well ordered, "decked with peace, and (the childe of peace) good husbandrie" (I, 14). In the course of Sidney's epic we are to watch the utopian government of Arcadia disintegrate into chaos, with the ideal landscape ravaged by beasts and civil war.

If the landscape is dependent upon the state, the state is dependent upon "the well tempered minds of the people" and their prince. The moral of the *Arcadia* is one of the great commonplaces of the Renaissance: private disorder breeds public tragedy.[1] The *Arcadia* opens with public tragedy brewing as a result of the king's virtual abdication, an act that has come about through his foolish surrender to fears concerning the oracle. Basilius' fears serve to initiate the story, but the characteristic source of disorder in the *Arcadia* is not fear but love. By the end of Book II, after Pyrocles has addressed the Arcadian rebels from the throne, Basilius' worry about the oracle has been quieted; now he remains in his retreat to continue his pursuit of Zelmane.

The *Arcadia* introduces the subject of love with the description of the passion of Strephon and Claius for the mysterious Urania, a shep-

---

[1] This theme is stated and discussed by Walter R. Davis, "A Map of Arcadia: Sidney's Romance in Its Tradition," in *Sidney's Arcadia* (New Haven: Yale University Press, 1965).

herdess whose name is probably intended to recall both the muse Urania, patron of divine contemplation, and Venus Urania, patron of heavenly love.[2] The passions of Strephon and Claius are as ideal and as far removed from the ordinary disorders of love as the landscape of Arcadia is from that of Laconia.

Hath not the onely love of her made us (being silly ignorant shepheards) raise up our thoughts above the ordinary levell of the worlde, so as great clearkes do not disdaine our conference? hath not the desire to seeme worthie in her eyes made us when others were sleeping, to sit vewing the course of heavens? when others were running at base, to runne over learned writings? when other marke their sheepe, we to marke our selves? hath not shee throwne reason upon our desires, and, as it were given eyes unto Cupid? (I, 7–8)

But the idyllic period of their life is over, for the opening of the *Arcadia* is not a celebration of Urania but a lament for her departure, and the two shepherds' pursuit of wisdom has yielded to sorrow and complaint. Strephon and Claius are no longer metaphorically or actually at home in the ideal landscape of Arcadia; significantly, when we first meet the bereaved shepherds they are standing upon the "wasted soile" of Laconia, having arrived there, as they explain, "guided with love" (I, 13–14). Later, in the double sestina "Yee Gote-heard Gods," they will take the Arcadian landscape as an image of their souls, recounting in detail how the departure of Urania has transformed "to desarts our best pastur'de mountaines." The tragedy described in the double sestina is more than the personal loss of two shepherds; as we shall see, all Arcadia has been transformed by the departure of Urania. So deprived, the land has become dark and foreboding, the "high and stately moun-

[2] For the most complete study of this subject, see Katherine D. Duncan-Jones, "Sidney's Urania," *Review of English Studies*, XVII (1966), 123–132.

THE ARCADIA

taines" have become "lowe dejected vallies," the forests have been "spoiled" and echo with the "dreadfull cries of murdred men." Venus Urania, mother of divine love, has forsaken Arcadia and only the earthly Venus, mother of the blind Cupid of passionate love, remains.[3]

The world of Sidney's *Arcadia* is thus the imperfect world of our own experience, the world of pressing moral problems rather than of the unalloyed harmony of the Arcadian ideal. The ultimate reason for Arcadia's fall from the ideal is, in Sidney's mythology, the departure of Urania. The goal toward which Arcadia aspires is to regain the ordered serenity of the pastoral ideal, to find some satisfactory substitute for Venus Urania. The vital fact about Urania was that she was able to throw "reason upon our desires," to give "eyes unto Cupid." The central problem for Sidney's forsaken characters is to recover this power, to find some way, in other words, of reconciling reason with passion.

From the active life of heroic endeavor, from valorous deeds amid the ravaged wastes of Laconia, Pyrocles, Prince of Macedonia, comes to Arcadia. The land he enters has already fallen somewhat from the ideal, but it has not yet disintegrated into the chaos of its neighbor. Arcadia is still a place of extraordinary peace and beauty, a country closer to perfection than to the condition of the rest of the world. Pyrocles is enraptured and believes he has discovered not merely something close to perfection but perfection itself:

Do you not see how all things conspire together to make this country a heavenly dwelling? Do you not see the grasse how in colour they excell the Emeralds, everie one striving to pass his fellow, and yet they are all kept of an equal height? And see you not the rest of these beau-

[3] Ringler, pp. 111–113. On the use of landscape in the double sestina, see David Kalstone, *Sidney's Poetry: Contexts and Interpretations* (Cambridge: Harvard University Press, 1965), pp. 9–39.

tifull flowers, each of which would require a mans wit to know, and his life to expresse? Do not these stately trees seeme to maintaine their florishing olde age with the onely happines of their seat, being clothed with a continuall spring, because no beautie here should ever fade? . . . Certainelie, certainely, cosin, it must needes be that some Goddesse enhabiteth this Region, who is the soule of this soile: for neither is any, lesse then a Goddesse, worthie to be shrined in such a heap of pleasures: nor any lesse then a Goddesse, could have made it so perfect a plotte of the celestiall dwellings. (I, 57)

The authentic goddess has left Arcadia; the goddess Pyrocles means is Philoclea, the younger daughter of Basilius. The sight of her beauty as captured in a portrait in Kalander's summer house has opened Pyrocles' eyes to the beauty of the landscape and has made the mundane appear divine. Musidorus, whose own vision has not yet been altered by love, perceives nothing celestial about Arcadia: "I marvell at the excessive praises you give to this countrie; in trueth it is not unpleasant: but yet if you would returne into Macedon, you should see either many heavens, or find this no more then earthly" (I, 58).

The ideal Pyrocles believes he has found in Arcadia is that of the life of contemplation. Like Strephon and Claius, the prince aspires to feed his mind with higher thoughts, to ascend to wisdom through love. He explains to Musidorus that his recent inaction and solitariness signify no slackening of his virtue, but the pursuit of a new kind of wisdom, "and in such contemplation, or as I thinke more excellent, I enjoye my solitarines; and my solitarines perchaunce is the nurse of these contemplations" (I, 56). Philoclea is to be Pyrocles' Urania; love of her, he hopes, will prepare him to turn his affections ultimately to heavenly love. "And in that heavenly love, since ther are two parts, the one the love it self, th'other the excellency of the thing loved; I, not

46

able at the first leap to frame both in me, do now (like a diligent workman) make ready the chiefe instrument, and first part of that great worke, which is love it self; which when I have a while practised in this sort, then you shall see me turn it to greater matters" (I, 80–81).

Life in Arcadia does not turn out as the idealistic prince expects. Instead of a land of peace and serenity, he finds a nation in the early stages of civil war, its countryside already beginning to suffer from the burnings and lootings of rebellious citizens. Instead of a love that raises him to the heights of contemplation, he discovers a passion that brings him the torments of a soul divided against itself. Even as Pyrocles debates with his cousin the virtues of contemplation and love, Sidney makes clear the impossibility of the ideal life to which the prince aspires. Already the disorder in his soul mocks his aspirations; his passion has wrought such internal chaos that he is unable even to produce a coherent argument in support of his new course. Pyrocles commences with a reasoned defense of his solitariness, but midway in the argument he suddenly halts in confusion and launches into his impassioned praise of the serene Arcadian landscape. Musidorus, Sidney tells us, "might perceive in him store of thoughts, rather stirred then digested; his words interrupted continually with sighes (which served as a burthen to each sentence) and the tenor of his speech (though of his wonted phrase) not knit together to one constant end, but rather dissolved in it selfe, as the vehemencie of the inwarde passion prevailed" (I, 57). Pyrocles' error has been his failure to comprehend the imperfect state of the world. Having encountered what seems to him divinity in the image of Philoclea, he has been led to suppose that Arcadia is indeed perfect and that he too is capable of realizing perfection in himself.

If Pyrocles misconceives the Arcadian reality by imagining it to be better than in fact it is, Musidorus, committed to an active life of heroism, ascribes to it less goodness than it actually possesses. In the Arcadian landscape he perceives nothing extraordinary, and in love of women he sees no good at all. Women to Musidorus are creatures of no virtue; admiration of them is "the very first downe-steppe to all wickednes." Passionate love is no more than sensuality, "engendered betwixt lust and idlenes," and "the matter it workes upon is nothing, but a certaine base weaknes, which some gentle fooles call a gentle hart." His counsel to Pyrocles is to regain control over this "sensuall weaknes" and return to the virtuous state: "Remember (for I know you know it) that if we wil be men, the reasonable parte of our soule, is to have absolute commaundement; against which if any sensuall weaknes arise, we are to yeelde all our sounde forces to the overthrowing of so unnaturall a rebellion" (I, 77–78). Musidorus' error is that he makes no satisfactory distinction between love and lust. All love of woman is lust to him, and there is no provision in his philosophy for such admirable, though earthly, lovers as Argalus and Parthenia.

In a somewhat different way, Musidorus is as much an idealist as Pyrocles. The elder prince's allegiance is to the humanist ideal of the reasonable and temperate man. In the course of his experiences in Arcadia, Pyrocles is to learn that the contemplative ideal is no longer possible and that love in an imperfect world has more in common with lust than he suspected. Similarly, Musidorus is to discover that his ideal of reason is not always easy to realize. Perhaps these are matters that the princes have frequently been told, but Sidney's point is that "all is but lip-wisdome, which wants experience" (I, 113). The *Arcadia* abounds with disputations in which opposite philosophies confront each other, but these debates are never resolved; not once does any speaker, with mere words, convert his opponent to his point of view. In Sidney's conception, only experience can truly instruct, and nothing in Musidorus' personal experience before arriving in Arcadia has led him to suspect that the maintenance of temperance in one's private life is a rather complex task. Actually he has had virtually no private life at all; his experiences have been almost solely in the world of public events. It is precisely because private virtue has always seemed an easy matter to him that he is so outraged when he discovers that his cousin has become an intemperate lover.

Before coming to Arcadia, Pyrocles and Musidorus proved themselves to be more than competent in public affairs. But, as we have seen, virtue in the public sphere is ultimately dependent upon virtue in one's private life, upon maintaining a well-tempered mind. "O no," writes the wise Philanax to Basilius, "he cannot be good, that knowes not why he is good, but stands so farre good, as his fortune may keepe him unassayed" (I, 26). So far the fortunes of the princes have kept them "unassayed" by the difficulties of the private life; now they are to be tested. In Arcadia they are to receive the completion of their education for lives as rulers of states—they are to discover by experience the slippery foundation upon which public virtues rest.

The opposition between the princes in the debates of Book I embodies the conflicting Elizabethan attitudes toward love, the humanist ethic of reason and the romantic idealization of passion. Musidorus' scorn for those "gentle fooles" who speak of the "gentle hart" (I, 78) constitutes a direct challenge to the literary and philosophical tradition reaching back to the troubadours. On the other side, Pyrocles' invocation of those "notable men" who have considered love to be the "highest power of the mind" (I, 80) is an appeal to the authority of the same tradition. One of Sidney's concerns in the *Arcadia* is to examine each of these attitudes in the context of the imperfect world of experience.

Passion in this world is a force of such power and its operation a process so inexorable that, in the face of its onslaught, corrupted reason stands little chance of victory. This is what Musidorus learns when he first sees Pamela. In the light of the discovery, his fine maxims seem now to the prince rather ridiculous, mere lip wisdom. Moreover, he has found that passionate love, whether or not it is a weakness, has much to commend it and that he "who will resist it, must either have no witte, or [have] put out his eyes." Before seeing Pamela, Musidorus argued that the distinguishing characteristic of mankind is reason, that "if we wil be men, the reasonable parte of our soule, is to have absolute commaundement." Now he finds that the essential distinction between man and beast is in the ability to perceive beauty: "Beasts onely cannot discerne beauty, and let them be in the role of Beasts that doo not honor it." Pyrocles twits his friend by recalling to him his own sayings. "Why how now deere cousin . . . you that were last day so hie in Pulpit against lovers, are you now become so meane an auditor? Remember that love is a passion; and that a woorthie mans reason must ever have the masterhood." But in this new context the pat sayings of the conventional moralists seem inadequate. "I recant, I recant (cried Musidorus,) and withall falling downe prostrate, O thou celestial, or infernal spirit of Love, or what other heavenly or hellish title thou list to have (for effects of both I finde in my selfe) have compassion of me, and let thy glory be as great in pardoning them that be submitted to thee, as in conquering those that were rebellious" (I, 113–114).

The overly idealistic lover is of course no less ludicrous in Sidney's world than the naive moralist. As he is debating in lofty terms about the virtues of love, earnestly defending himself from Musidorus' accusations that passionate love "doth . . . womanish a man" (I, 78), Pyrocles is wearing the ridiculous costume of an Amazon lady. This disguise has frequently been interpreted with great solemnity. One critic, for example, finds it "a touch of Sidneian allegory" intended to reveal the perfection of the prince, who unites in himself both the masculine and feminine virtues, and he commends Sidney for his "gravely beautiful handling of Pyrocles' dual nature." [4] The disguise is indeed a touch of allegory, although its meaning is rather different from what this statement would suggest. The Amazon, famous for her refusal to accept the authority of men, is a common emblem of the injustice of female rule. By subjecting himself to Philoclea and allowing his reason, the masculine element in his soul, to be overcome by his passion, the feminine element, Pyrocles has become an authentic Amazon, a living example of the truth of Musidorus' contention that passionate love effeminates a man. Still it is not the emblematic significance of the costume that first strikes the reader, but its absurdity. The image of the noble prince done up as a lady breeds both delight and laughter, as Sidney puts it in the *Defense of Poesie* with reference to a picture of Hercules in woman's clothes: "for the representing of so straunge a power in Love, procures delight, and the scornefulnesse of the action, stirreth laughter" (III, 40).

Because of their imperfect natures, there is a disparity between the lovers' idealistic professions and their actions, and sometimes this disparity brings the *Arcadia* very close to burlesque. In Book II, for example, Sidney gives us a scene in Gynecia's coach in which Pyrocles is seated next to Philoclea and becomes aroused by the physical contact, "for the narrownesse of the coach made them joine from the foote to the shoulders very close together; the truer touch wherof though it were barred by their envious apparell, yet as a perfect Magnes, though put in an ivorie boxe, will thorow the boxe send forth his imbraced

---

[4] John F. Danby, *Poets on Fortune's Hill: Studies in Sidney, Shakespeare, Beaumont & Fletcher* (London: Faber and Faber, 1952), pp. 56–57. On the iconography of this costume, see my "Sidney's Womanish Man," *Review of English Studies*, XV (1964), 353–363.

vertue to a beloved needle; so this imparadised neighbourhood made
Zelmanes soule cleave unto her, both thorow the ivory case of her body,
and the apparell which did over-clowd it." The simile of the magnet,
suggesting that the prince's desire is essentially spiritual, is at least
qualified by the context, which is hardly spiritual. Sidney is not denying that Pyrocles' soul may yearn for union with Philoclea's, but he is
suggesting that the prince's physical longing is at least as powerful as
his spiritual desire. The comedy of the scene is made explicit in the
following sentence, where Sidney tells how the prince's blood was
bubbling like sugared wine, how his heart was struggling like an imprisoned lion, and how he himself was "striving violently (if it had
bene possible) to have leapt into the lappe of Philoclea" (I, 166–167).
Elsewhere in Book II Pyrocles is fortunate enough to observe his lady
bathing naked in the river; once again his physical desire becomes so
intense that he can barely restrain himself. Gazing upon Philoclea's
beauty, the disguised Amazon "had the coales of her affection so
kindled with wonder, and blowne with delight, that nowe all her parts
grudged, that her eyes should doo more homage, then they, to the
Princesse of them." In this sensual context, Sidney wryly informs us
that the prince's "wit began to be with a divine furie inspired" (I, 218),
and the scene becomes a travesty of ideal love as Pyrocles sings the
voluptuous *blason* of Philoclea's delights. After more than a hundred
lines of the most vivid physical description, Pyrocles recalls

> *How all this is but a faire Inne*
> *Of fairer guest, which dwells within,*
> (*Ringler, p. 90*)

but it is apparent that the inn rather more than the guest has inspired
his divine fury.

THE ARCADIA

Sidney's point in both incidents, as in numerous other places in the *Arcadia*, is that in the imperfect world the pure metal of love has been alloyed by sensuality. The reality of love is not, as Musidorus had argued, sensuality alone; neither is love quite the noble desire that Pyrocles had wished. The *Arcadia*, like so many other Elizabethan works, is replete with echoes of the Neoplatonists, with references to divine furies and striving souls. It is not itself Neoplatonic in philosophy, however, and is actually a good-humored critique of the far-fetched notions of the idealists. Sidney's own mind is too sensible, has too powerful a grasp upon reality, ever to surrender wholly to the rapture of any divine fury. This is not to say that his mind is closed to the genuine divinity in man, but he is always aware that mankind is at least as comic as it is divine.

Sidney's vision of the imperfect world is comic, but not merely comic. The incidental stories that amplify the main plot, especially those of Book II, trace the more serious consequences of passion.[5] Fortunately, the loves of Pyrocles and Musidorus are suitable—Philoclea and Pamela are in both virtue and nobility appropriate objects for the princes' affections. The results of an unsuitable passion are illustrated in the story of Erona's love for the base Antiphilus, a passion that ends in misery for herself and disaster for her country. The disorders resulting from sheer lust are exemplified by Andromana, who gains control of and tyrannizes over the kingdom of Iberia. In the main plot, too, the

[5] On the relation of the incidental stories to the main plot, see Davis' "Map of Arcadia," pp. 114–135. See also Nancy Rothwax Lindheim, "Sidney's *Arcadia*, Book II: Retrospective Narrative," *Studies in Philology*, LXIV (1967), 159–186, who argues that the stories of Book II, beginning with examples of unambiguous moral choice, progressively become more complex, initiating the princes and the reader into a world in which the black and white of copybook morality has been replaced by the varied grays of reality.

53

graver side of passion is illustrated. Basilius' pursuit of Zelmane has serious effects on the state as well as a more ludicrous side in the king's private behavior. The chief example of the dreadful condition to which passion may reduce a noble mind is Gynecia. The queen's hopeless desire for Pyrocles has filled her soul with "wild ravenous beastes," has transformed her into a monstrous creature, the sworn enemy of her own daughter, whom she vows to murder rather than permit to enjoy the prince's love.

Gynecia's passion is of course intended to illustrate lust rather than true love, but in the world of the *Arcadia* the partitions that divide the two, virtuous desire and mere sensuality, are very thin indeed. Just how thin they are is made apparent in an important scene in Book III where, driven to distraction by his desire, Pyrocles withdraws to a dark cave and yields to "the weakenes of lamentation." [6] Throughout the *Arcadia* passionate love is associated with darkness, blindness, and night, and the dark cave embodies these qualities. Sitting before the cave, Pyrocles sings of how the effects of his passion are not what he had expected. Philoclea's radiance has paradoxically cast darkness instead of light upon his soul. To the prince's great surprise, his complaint is echoed by a lamentation from the depths of the cave. In the second singer he recognizes a kindred soul whom he vows to seek out, "for thy musique well assures me wee are at least-hand fellowe prentises to one ungracious master" (II, 9). The kindred soul turns out to be Gynecia, her powers wasted by lust and despair. Pyrocles' passion has reduced him to a state almost indistinguishable from hers.

If Pyrocles and Gynecia have so much in common, what distinction can be made in the *Arcadia* between love and lust? The point of the incident is, I believe, that so far as the state of mind of the individual

---

[6] On this scene, see Walter R. Davis, "Actaeon in Arcadia," *Studies in English Literature,* II (1962), 95–110.

is concerned, no satisfactory distinction can be made. Gynecia's disorders are more intense, more hellish, than Pyrocles', but they are kindred. In a world in which sensual desire has so strong a hold over even the most virtuous, the disorders of lust and the torments of love are nearly identical. Some fortunate few such as the remarkable Pamela may avoid the worst effects of love but, for the majority of mankind, to love at all is to enter a very questionable moral state. Moreover, whether he is to love or not is a matter over which the individual does not always have control. Cupid's arrow, as the example of Musidorus shows, can strike even the most unwilling and, once begun, the process of disintegration proceeds apace. In the face of this reality, any kind of idealism seems naive.

Yet, from a different point of view, Pyrocles and Musidorus have very little in common with Gynecia and Basilius, for the princes' affections are properly placed and their goal is marriage while the others' is adultery. To pursue virtuous desire in an imperfect world, however, is to enter upon a state as fraught with peril as any battle or campaign: on the one hand the lover must avoid the danger of melancholic despair and, on the other, lies the threat that, the distant goal forgotten, his passion may degenerate into lust. Pyrocles regards his love for Philoclea as a new manifestation of heroism. It is a figure of Hercules that he has chosen for his device, and for his motto he has taken the heroic phrase "Never more valiant." The brief note he writes when departing to seek Philoclea has the air of a resolved soldier going off to war: "My onely friend, violence of love leades me into such a course, wherof your knowledge may much more vexe you, then help me. Therefore pardon my concealing it from you, since: if I wrong you, it is in respect I beare you. Returne into Thessalia, I pray you, as full of good fortune, as I am of desire: and if I live, I will in short time follow you; if I die, love my memorie" (I, 61). These heroic pretentions may be laughable, but at the same time they are justified, for his embracing of love is truly an act of great daring. Disguised as an Amazon, the prince is fitted out for battle, and in Arcadia he will find battle, a civil war within the little state of his own soul. This is the paradoxical heroism of love as Sidney sees it, that in order to attain his virtuous goal the hero must dare to become metamorphosed into something less than himself, into a shepherd or an Amazon, a living image of the disorders of passion: "O heaven and earth (said Musidorus) to what a passe are our mindes brought, that from the right line of vertue, are wryed to these crooked shifts? But o Love, it is thou that doost it; thou changest name upon name; thou disguisest our bodies, and disfigurest our mindes. But in deed thou hast reason, for though the wayes be foule, the journeys end is most faire and honourable" (I, 117).

VIRTUE AND JUSTICE IN ARCADIA

Some recent criticism has held that the *Arcadia* is Sidney's Christian epic and that what the princes acquire in their experiences is the Christian virtue of patience.[1] Yet the heroes of the *Arcadia* are not Christians but pagan Greeks, worshipers of Apollo, Venus, Pan, and the other deities of ancient Greece. Milton understood this very well when he reminded the followers of the late King Charles that Pamela's

---

[1] See Danby, *Poets on Fortune's Hill*, pp. 46–73, and Davis, "Map of Arcadia," pp. 59–83. Davis' interpretation is the more comprehensive of the two. According to him, the princesses have been raised to moral perfection through their trials in captivity. The princes, as Pyrocles' attempts at suicide demonstrate, lack the Christian virtues, in which they are finally instructed by the princesses. In the course of the story, Pyrocles and Musidorus ascend a modified Platonic ladder and finally attain transcendental heights of Christian wisdom as in prison they meditate upon the afterlife. One of the difficulties with this reading is that, at the very end of the captivity episode, Pamela and Philoclea are themselves saved from suicide by Pyrocles.

56

prayer is the devotion of a woman who is but "a Heathen fiction praying to a heathen God." The rest of Milton's comment is better known. He calls the *Arcadia* "no serious Book" but a "vain amatorious Poem," a poem "in that kind full of worth and witt, but among religious thoughts, and duties not worthy to be nam'd; nor to be read at any time without good caution; much less in time of trouble and affliction to be a Christians Prayer-Book." [2] The most interesting words here are "in that kind full of worth and witt": Milton is not criticizing Charles for reading the *Arcadia*, which he evidently admires, but for imagining that it can be taken as a guide in matters of religion. The error that Sidney's more recent readers have been making has royal precedent, but it is still an error.

So far from intending a Christian epic, Sidney has conceived the *Arcadia* as a period piece, and he generally attempts to remain faithful to his pre-Christian period.[3] His conception of the differences between classical and modern cultures is not so well developed as our own, but he understands that the ancient world did differ from Elizabethan England. The matter of costume is typical: Sidney does not clothe his characters in doublets and hose, but in the kind of dress he believes the pagan Greeks actually wore. In Book V, for example, when the princes emerge from prison on the way to their trial, he describes in great detail how they are clothed "after the Greeke manner," lingering with obvious relish over even such minute points as the precise color of Musidorus' purple cloak. This was, he tells us, not "that purple which we now have," but "the right Tyrian purple, which was nearest

---

[2] *Eikonoklastes*, in *Prose Works*, III, ed. Merritt Y. Hughes (New Haven: Yale University Press, 1962), 362–363.

[3] Although some critics disapproved of Christian poets writing about pagan heroes, it was a commonplace of Renaissance theory that an epic should be set in a remote period. See, for example, Tasso, "Discourses," in Gilbert, *Literary Criticism*, pp. 479–482.

to a cullour betwixt our murrey and skarlet" (II, 169). In other matters, too, he is concerned to remind his audience that they are not
reading about modern characters. At the trial, Philoclea's punishment
for her imprudent behavior is to be confined to a house of religious
women, a nunnery in other words; however, Sidney specifies that these
are not Christian sisters but the "vestall nonnes" (II, 173).

There are of course many moments when Sidney shows little concern for his period, the most notable anachronisms occurring in the
several tilts replete with impresas and elaborate suits of armor.[4] In
matters of religious belief, however, historical perspective is fairly
consistently maintained. After being saved from the lion and the bear,
Basilius sings a hymn of thanks to Pan. And of the two most familiar
prayers in the Arcadia, one, Basilius', is directed specifically to Apollo
and the other, Pamela's, is couched in terms as vague and generalized
as Sidney can make them, directed merely to the "all-seeing Light, and
eternal Life of all things" (I, 382). Nowhere do these characters evince
knowledge of any specifically Christian tenet or mystery. There is no
reference in the Arcadia to Christ, to the Trinity, to grace, or to salvation. Pamela's religious beliefs as revealed in her prayer and her debate
with Cecropia are, from a Christian point of view, sound enough but
sadly limited. She understands that man is imperfect and requires
divine help. She knows there is a God, the creator of man and the

---

[4] It may seem novel to suggest that the Arcadia reveals any historical sense
whatever. The usual view is that expressed by Walter Allen, who says that
Sidney's epic, mixing chivalry with antiquity, is "a superb example of the Elizabethan lack of the historical sense"—The English Novel (London: Phoenix
House, 1954), p. 23. This kind of anachronism was defended by some Italian
critics, who maintained that the epic poet must be prepared to ignore many of
the crudities of the distant age he is describing and substitute more modern
practices so that his poem will suit the taste of readers accustomed to refinements
unknown to the ancients. See, for example, Giraldi Cinthio, "On the Composition
of Romances," in Gilbert, Literary Criticism, pp. 270–271.

world, and that this God is infinitely good, infinitely wise, and infinitely powerful. As for the universe, she knows that not chance but providence rules all things. This is all she knows. Neither Pamela nor any other character in the *Arcadia* possesses any knowledge that, to Sidney's mind, would be impossible for a virtuous pagan to obtain by the use of reason alone.[5]

Although the heroes of the *Arcadia* are not Christians, their philosophy nevertheless has worth and wit. At the very opening of his first debate with Pyrocles, Musidorus gives a good example of the wisdom he is capable of:

A mind wel trained and long exercised in vertue (my sweete and worthy cosin) doth not easily chaunge any course it once undertakes, but upon well grounded and well wayed causes. For being witnes to it selfe of his owne inward good, it findes nothing without it of so high a price, for which it should be altered. Even the very countenaunce and behaviour of such a man doth shew forth Images of the same constancy, by maintaining a right harmonie betwixt it and the inward good, in yeelding it selfe sutable to the vertuous resolution of the minde. (I, 55)

In the late sixteenth century this speech, with its familiar catchwords of "constancy" and "resolution," would instantly have identified its speaker as a Stoic, and readers would have understood that Sidney conceived his characters as wise pagans, subscribers to a philosophy not

---

[5] The first section of de Mornay's *Verité de la Religion Chrétienne*, translated by Sidney and Golding, is devoted to determining which truths can be obtained by unaided reason and then to establishing that the wisest men of all ages, both Christian and pagan, have consented to these truths. Every tenet of Pamela's faith is considered by de Mornay to be knowledge obtainable by reason, as may be seen in the first nineteen chapters of his treatise.

59

in itself Christian but in fundamental harmony with Christian thought.[6] The proof of virtue to the Stoic is the ability to face adversity with a constant mind, the ability impassively to endure what lesser spirits cannot. He abides tribulations because he knows that all outward evil is illusory, but his constancy is different from Christian patience in that he does not expect his suffering to be rewarded in heaven: virtue to him is its own reward. The foundation of his philosophy is the conviction that the cosmos is ruled by providence and that therefore nothing can be truly evil. Whoever thinks otherwise is a fool, for he is suffering from the one authentic evil—a passionate, disordered mind.

The philosophical core of the *Arcadia* is the debate between Pamela and Cecropia, in which the fundamental assumptions of the niece's philosophy are revealed in dramatic confrontation with the aunt's libertine views. Actually this debate is a version of the ancient philosophical struggle of the Stoics against, on the one hand, the Epicureans and, on the other, the skeptics. Cecropia fuses Epicureanism with skepticism, bases her philosophy on an appeal to nature (not the rational nature understood by the Stoics, but the debased nature of the concrete world), and casts over the whole system a lurid, Machiavellian coloring. The debate begins with a conversation about a purse Pamela is embroidering and about physical beauty. Cecropia's excessive praise of the purse and Pamela's beauty surprises the niece, who answers ironically that if her aunt values beauty so highly she ought not to defile it by treating her basely. However, it is not really beauty that Cecropia values but pleas-

---

[6] For good discussions of the revival of Stoicism in the sixteenth century, see Rudolph Kirk's essay in his edition of Justus Lipsius, *Two Books of Constancie,* trans. John Stradling (New Brunswick: Rutgers University Press, 1939), pp. 3–62, and Herschel Baker, *The Dignity of Man: Studies in the Persistence of an Idea* (Cambridge: Harvard University Press, 1947), pp. 301–312. Gilbert Murray's *The Stoic Philosophy* (New York: Putnam, 1915) is still a suggestive introduction to the general mode of Stoic thought.

ure; she esteems beauty only for the power it confers in procuring delight. She urges Pamela to marry Amphialus and to do it immediately, that is, to make use of her power quickly before it is devoured by time. But Pamela replies that to marry Amphialus hastily and without her father's consent would be an offense to God, who "claimes at my hands obedience." Now Cecropia reveals the skepticism that underlies her Epicureanism and makes it possible: belief in God, she contends, is founded upon no more than opinion, and Pamela must not be fooled by "these bugbeares of opinions. . . . Be wise, and that wisedome shal be a God unto thee; be contented, and that is thy heaven." The truth is "that all things follow but the course of their own nature, saving only Man, who while by the pregnancie of his imagination he strives to things supernaturall, meane-while he looseth his owne naturall felicitie." Cecropia's philosophy is a direct assault upon the foundations of Pamela's Stoicism, the belief in providence and in a rational, ordered nature. Understanding that her aunt's position implies the Epicurean cosmology, Pamela responds with a fierce attack on the view that the universe was created by chance. Cecropia's skepticism she refutes with the argument from design, calling all her aunt's "senses to witnes" that they "can heare, nor see nothing, which yeeldes not most evident evidence" of God. Because Cecropia's conception of the cosmos is wrong, her notion of man's nature is also perverse: to follow nature means to live according to reason, not to indulge oneself in sensual delight. From the Stoic point of view, one is either *sapiens* or *stultus*, a sage or a fool. Cecropia is of course a fool, "and most miserably foolish, since wit makes you foolish" (I, 405–409).[7]

[7] Much scholarship has been devoted to elucidating the background and sources of this debate. The best discussion of the background is to be found in an article not directly concerned with Sidney, Louis I. Bredvold's "The Naturalism of Donne in Relation to Some Renaissance Traditions," *Journal of English and Germanic Philology*, XXII (1923), 471–502. See also Edwin Greenlaw, "The

This debate establishes the philosophical poles between which Sidney's characters move. As these characters leave the virtuous state of reason and begin to pursue their sensual desires, we find them acting as if they are adherents of Cecropia's perverse philosophy; they are ceasing to be wise men and becoming fools. The aunt's praise of beauty echoes Musidorus' sentiments. To man only, she says, "is given the judgement to discerne Beautie" (I, 403). According to Musidorus, "Beasts onely cannot discerne beauty, and yet them be in the role of Beasts that doo not honor it" (I, 113). By beauty, however, Cecropia understands only physical beauty; the prince means spiritual beauty as it is revealed in the physical. But to the extent that Musidorus forgets his true goal, to that extent he is behaving like an Epicurean and a skeptic.

The connection between passionate love and the Cecropian philosophy is made clear in the figure of Basilius. In Gynecia, Sidney wished to portray the dreadful psychological disorder of one given over to lust. No matter how completely she dedicates herself to vice, Gynecia never forgets what virtue is; indeed she continually torments herself with reflections upon her moral depravity. Partially because she has not forgotten virtue, Sidney generally treats her with dignity. Basilius, however, is a character apprehended intellectually rather than emotionally. Having yielded first to fear and then to lust, he is Sidney's principal example of the *stultus* and consequently is treated with no dignity

---

Captivity Episode in Sidney's *Arcadia*," in *The Manly Anniversary Studies* (Chicago: University of Chicago Press, 1923), pp. 54–63; Lois Whitney, "Concerning Nature in *The Countesse of Pembrokes Arcadia*," *Studies in Philology*, XXIV (1927), 207–222; Ronald B. Levinson, "The 'Godlesse Minde' in Sidney's *Arcadia*," *Modern Philology*, XXIX (1931), 21–26; Constance Miriam Syford, "The Direct Source of the Pamela-Cecropia Episode in the *Arcadia*," *PMLA*, XLIX (1934), 472–489; and D. P. Walker, "Ways of Dealing with Atheists: A Background to Pamela's Refutation of Cecropia," *Bibliothèque D'Humanisme et Renaissance*, XVII (1955), 252–277.

at all. In his wooing of Zelmane, the king reveals that love has turned him into an Epicurean and a skeptic, using the same catchwords of "opinion" and "nature" and the same kind of arguments that Cecropia had earlier used with Pamela. "Alas," he says with reference to chastity and virtue, "let not certaine imaginatife rules, whose trueth standes but upon opinion, keepe so wise a mind from gratefulnes and mercie, whose never failing laws nature hath planted in us." And later he dismisses the bond of his marriage pledge to Gynecia by claiming that mere "opinion" of the worth of such pledges ought not to prevent him from "paying the right duties to nature and affection" (II, 43, 92). Basilius' passion results in his ultimately taking the physical object of his desire for a god. He presents Zelmane with this poem:

> *Phaebus farewell, a sweeter Saint I serve,*
> *The high conceits thy heav'nly wisedomes breed*
> *My thoughts forget: my thoughts, which never swerve*
> *From her, in whome is sowne their freedome's seede,*
> *And in whose eyes my daily doome I reede.*
>
> *Phaebus farewell, a sweeter Saint I serve.*
> *Thou art farre off, thy kingdome is above:*
> *She heav'n on earth with beauties doth preserve.*
> *Thy beames I like, but her cleare rayes I love:*
> *Thy force I feare, her force I still do prove.*
>
> *Phaebus yeelde up thy title in my minde.*
> *She doth possesse, thy Image is defaste,*
> *But if thy rage some brave revenge will finde,*
> *On her, who hath in me thy temple raste,*
> *Employ thy might, that she my fires may taste.*
> >*And how much more her worth surmounteth thee,*
> >*Make her as much more base by loving me.*
> >>(Ringler, p. 72)

63

HEROIC LOVE

The passion of love does not reduce Pyrocles and Musidorus to the depths of Gynecia and Basilius, but it does disfigure their minds with unseemly laments and complaints, substituting for their virtuous resolution the familiar emotions of lovers—fear, shame, doubt, grief, and hope. Paradoxically, it is the same passion of love that is finally responsible for the princes' restoration to virtue. In Book IV, when he and Philoclea have been discovered in her chamber, Pyrocles realizes that his pursuit of desire has resulted in a disastrous situation in which his beloved will probably be executed. At this moment the prince, "his excellent wit strengthened with vertue but guided by love" (II, 104), rises to the occasion and heroically resolves to kill himself in order to save Philoclea's life. Gone from his soul is the selfishness and self-pity of the lover seeking satisfaction of his desire; his passion, for the moment at least, has become something wholly selfless, something to Sidney's mind compatible with reason.

According to several recent critics, Pyrocles' resolution to kill himself represents his moral nadir, "an extreme falling-away from the frame of patience—a final sin." [8] But the Greek prince is not to be judged by Christian standards, and Sidney, emphasizing Pyrocles' "well disposed minde" and "unshaked magnanimity," shows no intention to do so. Pyrocles' present resolution is to be contrasted with his earlier attempt at suicide when, a captive in Cecropia's castle, he was "caried with the madnes of anguish," believing Philoclea to have been executed (I, 483). Then he had yielded to his passion, crying out upon "tyraunt heaven" and "blinde providence"; now it is with Stoic impassivity that he resolves to take his life in order to save Philoclea's. Indifferent to everything but honor and the welfare of his beloved, Pyrocles is displaying the kind of virtue that Pamela and Philoclea demonstrate at

[8] Danby, *Poets on Fortune's Hill,* p. 66. See also Davis, "Map of Arcadia," pp. 80–81.

64

the end of their long trial of fortitude in Cecropia's castle, when, believing themselves in the power of the lustful brothers Anaxius and Zoilus, the sisters resolve to take their own lives. As Pamela then says, "it becomes our birth to thinke of dying nobly, while we have done, or suffered nothing, which might make our soule ashamed at the parture from these bodies." The princesses are prevented from suicide by Pyrocles who, commending Pamela's principles, rejects her analysis of the situation. "Vertuous and faire Ladie (said Zelmane) what you say is true; and that truth may well make up a part in the harmonie of your noble thoughts. But yet the time (which ought alwayes to be one) is not tuned for it; while that may bring foorth any good, doo not barre your selfe thereof: for then would be the time to die nobly, when you can not live nobly" (I, 508). Now, with Philoclea's life endangered, Pyrocles believes the time is finally ripe for suicide, for, as he sees it, his own death is the only event that may bring forth any good.

But before the prince can achieve his end, Philoclea awakens and turns out to be as unwilling to live without Pyrocles as he is to allow her to forfeit her life. What Pyrocles has forgotten is that the lady is in her own way as resolute as he: "For she, not with an unshaked magnanimity, wherewith Pyrocles wayed and dispised death, but with an innocent guiltlessnes, not knowing why she should feare to deliver her unstained soule to God . . . did almost bring her minde to as quiet attending all accidents, as the unmastred vertu of Pyrocles" (II, 107). The lovers now engage in a formal debate in which Philoclea, repeating sayings of "wise men," argues against suicide as Pyrocles defends his intention. This debate should not be taken as a confrontation of truth and error in which the lady, like Redcross' Una, acts as Pyrocles' guide, educating him in Christian virtue. Philoclea's motive is not to save her lover's soul but his life, and to do so she is bringing forth every argument she has ever heard against suicide, preferring by far

65

that they should both be destroyed at the hands of the law. Her presentation of the case against suicide does not sway his resolution. Once again Pyrocles is about to take his life when she intervenes to swear that, if he perseveres, she will not only mutilate her body but destroy herself in so terrible a manner "as she might think the paine of it would countervaile the never dying paine of her minde." Convinced that she is in earnest, and understanding therefore that his death will not preserve her life, Pyrocles "retired himselfe, with as much tranquillitie from it, as before he had gone unto it. Like a man, that had set the keeping or leaving of the bodye, as a thing without himselfe, and so had thereof a freed and untroubled consideracion" (II, 112–113). The debate between Pyrocles and Philoclea, culminating as it does in the lady's own threat of suicide, is not so much a struggle between different points of view on self-destruction as it is a display on each side of fortitude and magnanimity. We have witnessed this kind of heroic love once before in the *Arcadia*, in the persons of Argalus and Parthenia.

One of Philoclea's recurring arguments is that Pyrocles' determination cannot be virtuous since it must proceed from some passion; if his resolve does not spring from fear or despair, then it must come "of some other disguised passion" (II, 111). The lady is correct: Pyrocles' resolve does proceed from a passion, love. Sidney is demonstrating that orthodox Stoicism must be qualified by the recognition that not every passion is necessarily evil. The passion of love may take many forms: it may be basely sensual, as in the case of Basilius and Gynecia, or it may be a mixed love, a passion of both body and mind, as in the case of the princes. And in a noble soul this mixed passion, at some times almost indistinguishable from lust, may at other times produce the most admirable effects of virtue. What Sidney has done is to reconcile the two traditions: he has revealed that love may result in the kind of behavior even a Stoic would approve. This is the common denominator between Stoicism and the medieval romantic tradition—each insists that the good life is attainable only by the noble. The *Arcadia* is hardly democratic. In Sidney's conception the noble alone are capable of love and virtue: those of humble birth, such as the ignorant Arcadian rebels or the cowardly Dametas and his slatternly family, he consistently treats with ridicule and scorn. Infected with sensuality, Pyrocles and Musidorus have called into question the nobility of their spirits. Appropriately, Musidorus' disguise in Arcadia is as a humble shepherd, and before Pamela will attend to his suit, the prince must convince her that he is not truly base. Such proof is required of Pyrocles and Philoclea too, and in their debate Sidney gives us that proof. It is the final confirmation that each lover is worthy of the other.

Simultaneously with the discovery of Pyrocles in Philoclea's chamber, Basilius' lifeless body is found at the cave and Musidorus, having attempted to flee with Pamela, is captured and brought back to the royal lodge. Seeing Musidorus a prisoner and himself but just restored to virtue, Pyrocles is uncertain of the state of his cousin's mind. "O my Palladius saide he, let not our vertue now abandon us; let us prove our mindes are no slaves to fortune, but in adversitie can triumph over adversitie." Pyrocles need have no doubts. In the moment of crisis, Musidorus' nobility has also reasserted itself: "Deere Daiphantus aunsweared Musidorus . . . I thanke you for this best care of my best parte. But feare not, I have kept too long company with you to want nowe a thorowe determination of these things, I well know there is nothing evill but within us, the rest is either naturall or accidentall" (II, 129).

To the Arcadians, the situation—in which two strange noblemen are discovered with the royal princesses on the same morning that Basilius is found dead—has the appearance of a plot to take over the state, and Pyrocles and Musidorus are put in prison to await trial. In prison the princes do not, as has been suggested, ascend to transcendental heights of contemplation; rather, expecting death, they fortify their spirits by recalling those Stoic truths which had been the common furniture of their minds. They reflect upon providence, considering how there is "nothing done by the unreachable ruler . . . but hath an everlasting reason for it," and they remind themselves how "bodely mischiefes . . . be but mischiefes to the baser mindes, too much delighted with the kennell of this life" (II, 164). In order to confirm their resolution, they consider how after death their immortal souls will be free from that sensual weakness which in this life has so troubled them. Their meditations are recapitulated in Musidorus' sonnet, which is not a new composition but one "he had made before love turned his muse to another subjecte."

> *Since nature's workes be good, and death doth serve*
> *As nature's worke: why should we feare to die?*
> *Since feare is vaine, but when it may preserve,*
> *Why should we feare that which we cannot flye?*
>
> *Feare is more paine, then is the paine it feares,*
> *Disarming humane mindes of native might:*
> *While each conceate an ouglie figure beares,*
> *Which were not evill, well vew'd in reason's light.*
>
> *Our owly eyes, which dimm'd with passions bee,*
> *And scarce discerne the dawne of comming day,*
> *Let them be clearde, and now begin to see,*
> *Our life is but a step in dustie way.*

THE ARCADIA

Then let us holde the blisse of peacefull minde,
Since this we feele, great losse we cannot find.[9]

"Thus," Sidney says, "did they like quiet Swannes, sing their own obsequies, and vertuously enhable their mindes against all extremities, which they did thinke woulde fall uppon them" (II, 166). Now, returned to the virtuous state, the princes remove their demeaning disguises and assume their proper costumes. Love had cast them into the darkened prison of sensuality. But their sleeping nobility has awakened, and they emerge from prison steadfast and resolved, restored once again to their true selves.

Rehabilitated though they are, Pyrocles and Musidorus must yet be called to account for their transgressions. In strict justice, neither their present nor their previous virtue can be allowed to obscure their ill behavior during most of their stay in Arcadia: "no man," says Euarchus, "because he hath done well before, should have his present evils spared, but rather so much the more punished, as having shewed he knew how to be good" (II, 196). And in the court of Euarchus, the princes receive absolute and unmitigated justice, according to the letter of the law of Greece and Arcadia. The judge is the very model of reason. Attending to the arguments of Philanax and the princes,

---

[9] Ringler, p. 131. According to Davis, this poem's "structural procedure is one of transcendence" as "the struggles of the moral life fade before the slow opening up of the glorious light of heaven" ("Map of Arcadia," pp. 66–67). The procedure of this sonnet seems to me rather one of argument and conclusion, with the first twelve lines designed to lead to the Stoic resolution of the couplet. The octave presents the arguments for the Stoic point of view; the third quatrain is an exhortation to accept that point of view; and the couplet, assuming that the exhortation has been successful, proves the correctness of the decision by describing the benefits of Stoic resolution.

Euarchus "shewed in his face no motions, either at the ones or other speeche, letting passe the flowers of rhetoricke, and onely marking whether their reasons tended" (II, 194). His own speech pronouncing judgment is an example of precise legal reasoning, couched in a style stripped and bare, appealing wholly to the intellect.[10]

Euarchus' judgment is that Pyrocles and Musidorus have been at least accidentally involved in Basilius' death; however, their principal crime is the ravishing of the princesses, "for though they ravished them not from themselves, yet they ravished them from him that owed them, which was their father. An acte punished by all the Graecian lawes, by the losse of the head, as a most execrable theft." The princes attempt to explain their behavior by reminding the court of the irresistible power of love, but Euarchus replies that true love "can never slide into any action that is not vertuous": their desires are not love at all but merely lusts they ought to have restrained. Rather than be executed, the princes say, they ought to be married to the princesses. Euarchus' position is that wedlock, the foundation of society, cannot be set on a basis of lust, and "to allowe a patterne of such procurations of marriage" would produce social chaos (II, 196–197).

What Euarchus does is to uphold the absolute claims of reason, making no allowance whatever for human imperfection. In an ideal world, true love could never slide into vice. In an ideal world, parental authority would be exercised with wisdom and restraint. In an imperfect world, however, even the most virtuous must sometimes resort to desperate devices. Pamela, for example, is doubtless a lady of extraordinary prudence and wisdom. Virtuous not merely from innocence, like Philoclea, but from a knowledge of the foundations of

[10] On the various styles of the speeches in the *Arcadia*, see Lorna Challis, "The Use of Oratory in Sidney's *Arcadia,*" *Studies in Philology,* LXII (1965), 561–576.

goodness, the elder sister never surrenders to the extreme disorders of passion. Her love for Musidorus, based not so much upon his person as upon the proofs he offers of his rank and virtue, is of a kind Euarchus would thoroughly commend. Her deportment as Cecropia's captive is a model of steadfastness, and in her debate with Cecropia, when her aunt proposes the match with Amphialus, she points out the importance of parental approval in marriage. Yet not even Pamela can maintain a wholly virtuous course. Her father's unreasonable behavior, his restraint of her liberty and his strange humors, finally convince her that "contrarie to all generall rules of reason" (II, 23), she must elope with Musidorus, an act of which Euarchus can hardly approve.

Euarchus' judgment upon the princes is just but, given the nature of the world, far from equitable. The issue at the trial finally comes down to the question of equity or mercy versus justice or law, a matter with which the Elizabethans were much concerned. "In the extremest interpretation," Musidorus argues, their crime is "but a humaine error" and one which may, by permitting the marriages, be turned to profit for everyone concerned. He advises Euarchus not to "burne your house to make it cleane, but like a wise father, turne even the fault of your children to any good that may come of it." Strict adherence to law may, while seeking to maintain the abstract principles of justice unimpaired, disregard the true purpose of law, which is "to preserve, and not to destroy mankinde" (II, 193). Musidorus' speech is a plea for equity, for following the spirit rather than the letter of the law. Yet Philanax had warned that only Basilius, the king, possessed the "power to have mercy." From the protector who sits in his place, the accused must "looke for none other, then that which dead pittilesse lawes may allot unto you" (II, 117). Euarchus confirms this warning, asserting that although it might be convenient for the princes and princesses to marry, his function is not to determine "what were convenient for the parties" but only "what is juste in the never changing justice" (II, 197). Not even when he finds that the princes he has condemned are his own son and nephew does Euarchus temper his judgment; his allegiance is wholly to sacred justice, and before the law all merely private considerations must give place.[11]

Euarchus is admirable—his is an extraordinary zeal for virtue—and yet it is not to this idealist that Sidney gives the final word. The *Arcadia* concludes with the sudden awakening of Basilius, who steps from his bier to dispense the necessary clemency. This abrogation of the law has generally been interpreted as a serious flaw in the moral purpose of the *Arcadia*.[12] In fact it represents the triumph of equity over law, the accommodation of justice to the actual circumstances of the world. Recognizing that "in all these matters his owne fault had been the greatest," Basilius, "to the inestimable joy of Euarchus," arranges the marriages of the princes and princesses, thereby assuring that their love will not again decline from virtue. Understanding that the oracle has at last been fulfilled, Basilius realizes that all the events

[11] The relationship between common law and equity was the crucial legal question of the sixteenth century. The issue interested Spenser, who touches on it in various places in Book V of *The Faerie Queene*, and also Shakespeare, who deals with it in the trial scene in *The Merchant of Venice*. On Shakespeare's treatment, see Mark Edwin Andrews, *Law versus Equity in "The Merchant of Venice"* (Boulder: University of Colorado Press, 1965). In distinguishing between the powers of the protector and those of the king, the *Arcadia* reflects the theory of equity. It was the prerogative of the king, acting through his chancellor, the keeper of the king's conscience, to set the common law aside to assure equity. Sidney carries this principle one logical step further, assuming that if the king does not exist—a legal impossibility, of course—then there is no one to whom the accused can appeal for equity. For the classic exposition of the early theory of equity, see Christopher St. German's *Doctor and Student*, originally published under Henry VIII and many times reprinted throughout the sixteenth century.

[12] Ringler, for example, says it "completely undercuts the heroic adherence of Euarchus to 'sacred Rightfulnes'" and suggests that Sidney intended to alter the charges against the princes in order to resolve the moral ambiguity (*Poems*, p. 379).

in Arcadia have "fallen out by the highest providence" (II, 206). Indeed, the hand of providence has been evident throughout, divine mercy tempering strict justice, divine goodness repeatedly averting the disasters of man's infected reason, divine wisdom arranging for all the actors in this tragicomedy of love an education in their own weaknesses and in the foundations of virtue.

III
THE
FAERIE
QUEENE

LOVE IN THE FAERIE QUEENE

Love is for Spenser a metaphor, a narrative device for treating a broad range of subjects, as well as an interesting subject itself. The legend of holiness, for example, is cast in the form of a love story, the romance of the Redcross Knight and Una. But the subject of this romance, no matter how it is defined, is something other than the love of a man for a woman. In the romance of Britomart and Artegall, love ceases to be a metaphor and is treated in its own right, and it is with this important story that I shall be primarily concerned.

The largest part of the tale is presented in Book III, the book of chastity, but some aspects of the romance seemed to the poet to belong more properly under the headings of friendship and justice. As a follower of Ovid and Petrarch, Spenser regarded love as a war between the sexes, a discord to be resolved in marriage. Thus the battles between Britomart and Artegall, which lead to the concord of their betrothal, come in Book IV, where the general subject is friendship or concord. As a humanist and a Christian, Spenser believed that the traditional inversion of the sexes in love—the situation in which the man is the servant instead of the lord of his lady—involved an injustice. This aspect of love he logically reserved for Book V, the book of justice, where he deals with it in the story of Britomart's rescue of Artegall from the Amazon Radigund.

Although Books IV and V were not published until 1596, six years after Book III first appeared, it is likely that the romance of Britomart and Artegall was composed as a unit about fifteen years earlier, precisely at the time Sidney was writing and revising the *Arcadia*. It seems that Spenser's original conception of his work was not a poem divided into books, each with its own hero and subject, but a sprawling romantic epic like the *Orlando furioso* in which the main narrative thread would be the romance of Britomart and Artegall, patterned after Ariosto's principal story, the romance of Bradamante and Ruggiero.

HEROIC LOVE

Ariosto's tale had been intended as a compliment to the House of Este, and, likewise, the romance of Britomart and Artegall was evidently intended as a compliment to the Dudleys, the family of Spenser's patron, the Earl of Leicester, and of his friend, Philip Sidney. Probably it was some portion of this original romantic epic that the young poet submitted to Gabriel Harvey's censure in 1580, a narrative in which he was striving, according to Harvey, to "overgo" Ariosto.[1]

In the romance of Britomart and Artegall the English poet was remarkably faithful to the spirit of the *Orlando,* as he understood it. Spenser's view of Ariosto was not, however, the same as our own. In the latter part of the sixteenth century, Ariosto was read more for wisdom than wit, and to the Elizabethans the story of Bradamante and Ruggiero was a grave discussion of the morality of love. According to John Harington,

Bradamant is a perfect patterne of true honourable love to Rogero, moved first by his value, by his courage, by his behaviour, by his worth, which made him worthy of her love. In her you shall finde no rashnesse, no want of constancie, of faith, of all other due regardes: for neither could her sundrie overthwart chaunces, neither the expectation and length of time, (which is wont to breed alterations,) nor the obstinate covetousnesse of her father, nor the vaine ambition of her mother, nor the state and Empire of Leon, with all the promised riches and treasures his Father and he possessed, once withdraw her minde from

---

[1] On Spenser's composition, see W. J. B. Owen, "The Structure of *The Faerie Queene,*" *PMLA,* LXVIII (1953), 1079–1100. Owen's theory of the poem's growth, in my opinion, replaces that suggested by Josephine Waters Bennett in *The Evolution of "The Faerie Queene"* (Chicago: University of Chicago Press, 1942). On the relationship of the story of Britomart and Artegall to that of Bradamante and Ruggiero, see *Var.* III, 367–376. Mrs. Bennett discusses the complimentary nature of Spenser's story (*Evolution,* pp. 80–100; also Owen, p. 1095). For Harvey's comment, see the Spenser-Harvey correspondence in *Var. Prose Works,* p. 471.

her first love. Further, Bradamant did not rashlie fall in love, as did Olympia, but the Prophetesse Melissa, and tokens from above, did encourage her to her honest love, forshowing her of her noble posteritie, and of all those blessings that accompanie the same: so as indeed, in her onelie, we have a patterne of honest and commendable love before marriage.[2]

So, too, Spenser's Britomart is notable for her constancy and lack of rashness. Neither the "expectation and length of time" nor the temptations of Malecasta can withdraw her mind from her first love, Artegall. Just as Bradamante received "tokens from above," so in Merlin's cave Britomart receives similar tokens, "forshowing her of her noble posteritie" and encouraging her honest love. As we shall see, Spenser intended his heroine to stand, like Bradamante, as a "patterne of honest and commendable love before marriage." In the story of Britomart and Artegall the English poet, wishing to overgo Ariosto, has given us his own discussion of the morality of love.

BRITOMART IN LOVE

The first three and a half cantos of Book III constitute a section of *The Faerie Queene* more or less complete in itself and devoted almost entirely to love. It is in these cantos that Spenser introduces Britomart and develops the significance of her passion for Artegall. The poet does not present his narrative in chronological order, but gives us first his heroine's adventures at Castle Joyous and then, in a lengthy flashback, her earlier experiences in love, the inception of her passion, and her

---

[2] "A Briefe and Summarie Allegorie of Orlando Furioso," in Harington's Ariosto, sig. Mm5ʳ. On sixteenth-century interpretations of Ariosto, see Susannah Jane McMurphy, *Spenser's Use of Ariosto for Allegory*, University of Washington Publications in Language and Literature, II (Seattle, 1924).

visit to Merlin's cave. The section concludes with the end of the flashback and Britomart's encounter with Marinell on the seashore. In the conviction that Spenser had sound reasons for not adhering to chronological order in these cantos, I shall discuss the narrative events in the same order.[1]

At the start of Book III we find the poet seeking to forge a link between this and the preceding book, similar to that joining Books I and II. In the first canto of Book II Guyon and Redcross, as a result of Archimago's deceit, nearly come to blows. At the opening of Book III Britomart and Guyon do in fact fight, and the knight of temperance is thrown from his horse. The most familiar interpretation of this encounter is perhaps that of Frederick M. Padelford, who thinks the incident was intended to establish the superiority of the Christian virtue of chastity over its pagan counterpart, temperance. This reading presents some difficulties, for, even if temperance is a pagan virtue, Guyon, who speaks of "my Redeemer's death" (II.i.27), is evidently a Christian. Furthermore, it is unlikely that Spenser conceived of chastity as an exclusively Christian virtue. Probably he subscribed to the Protestant doctrine that marriage itself is not an exclusively Christian act and therefore no sacrament. Nor is it possible, especially at this early moment in her story, absolutely to identify Britomart with chastity. Britomart is not chastity personified; rather, as Spenser tells us, she is "the flowre of chastity" (III.xi.6)—that is, a chaste woman, just as Redcross is a holy man and certainly not, at the start of his story at any rate, holiness incarnate.[1]

---

[1] Britomart's sudden appearance and victory are reminiscent of the chance encounter in which Bradamante first appears and overthrows Sacripante in *Orlando furioso*, I.60ff. For Padelford's interpretation, see *Var*. III, 323–324. A. S. P. Woodhouse also believes it unlikely that Spenser conceived of chastity as a specifically Christian virtue. See "Nature and Grace in *The Faerie Queene*," ELH, XVI (1949), 213.

THE FAERIE QUEENE

A cautionary word or two about the nature of Spenser's allegory may be in order. "Allegory" was a word used more loosely in the Renaissance than it is today. Although many Elizabethan definitions imply something like our own sense of the term—a narrative with a systematic double meaning—other documents suggest that the word was also used for things we would call irony and proverb. What the early commentators on Ariosto refer to as his allegory is often what we would call the moral of the story. These commentators do not generally see the characters as embodiments of vices and virtues, but as human beings exemplary of vicious or virtuous actions. Similarly, in English criticism of the sixteenth century no sharp distinction seems to have been made between formal allegory and characters merely exemplary. That Spenser was among those who made no such distinction is apparent from his letter to Raleigh in which he glides easily from referring to his work as a "continued Allegory, or darke conceit" to speaking of the "profite of the ensample." He uses the letter to announce that *The Faerie Queene* is an epic in the tradition of "all the antique Poets historicall," poets he seems to understand as teaching more by examples than by what we would call allegory. We should notice, too, that when he comes to speak of his own heroes Spenser uses words that are ambiguous and may with equal likelihood be interpreted to mean that his knights are embodiments of virtues or that they are exemplary. He speaks of his three books thus: "The first of the knight of the Redcrosse, in whome I expresse Holines: The seconde of Sir Guyon, in whome I sette forth Temperaunce: The third of Britomartis a Lady knight, in whome I picture Chastity." [2]

[2] For Spenser's comments, see "A Letter of the Authors," *Var.* I, 167–168. On Elizabethan conceptions of allegory, see Joshua McClennan, *On the Meaning and Function of Allegory in the English Renaissance*, University of Michigan Contributions in Modern Philology, No. 6 (Ann Arbor, 1947), esp. pp. 2–8, and on Ariosto's commentators, McMurphy, *Spenser's Use of Ariosto*, pp. 11–23.

HEROIC LOVE

We must be wary, then, not to oversimplify *The Faerie Queene* by immediately reducing every one of the knights to a flat allegorical tag. We become acquainted gradually with the qualities of the characters by their actions, as well as by what the poet progressively tells us about them. I emphasize this because, although by the start of Book III we know a great deal about Sir Guyon and can hardly avoid associating him with temperance, we do not yet know very much about Britomart. A stranger, when first she gallops into sight we do not even know that she is a woman. We are seeing her from the point of view of Guyon, who naturally assumes his opponent is a man, and therefore Spenser uses the masculine pronoun for her. Only after Guyon has been thrown are we told that his defeat is due to an enchanted spear, a mysterious "secret powre," that the knight possesses. But what this power is, and why the stranger should be the enemy of a character strongly associated with temperance, we can yet have no idea. Spenser goes on, however, and, addressing himself to Guyon, provides the information required to understand the encounter we have just witnessed.

> *But weenedst thou what wight thee overthrew,*
> *Much greater griefe and shamefuller regret*
> *For thy hard fortune then thou wouldst renew,*
> *That of a single damzell thou wert met*
> *On equall plaine, and there so hard beset;*

For excellent essays on the nature of Spenser's allegory, see A. C. Hamilton, *The Structure of Allegory in "The Faerie Queene"* (Oxford: Oxford University Press, 1961), pp. 1–58, and Graham Hough, *A Preface to "The Faerie Queene"* (London: Duckworth, 1962), pp. 100–137. Hamilton emphasizes the exemplary nature of Spenser's characters as well as the danger of discarding the literal level and merely translating the story into abstract terms. Hough emphasizes the discontinuous nature of Spenser's allegory. See also the fine essay by Thomas P. Roche, Jr., in *The Kindly Flame: A Study of the Third and Fourth Books of Spenser's "Faerie Queene"* (Princeton: Princeton University Press, 1964), pp. 3–31.

THE FAERIE QUEENE

Even the famous Britomart it was,
Whom straunge adventure did from Britaine fet,
To seeke her lover (love farre sought alas,)
Whose image she had seene in Venus looking glas.
(III.i.8)

Nothing is said in this stanza about Britomart as the representative of chastity; the important fact revealed is that she is a lady famous for her adventures in love. That chastity should be at odds with temperance would be an extraordinary doctrine for Spenser to teach, but that a passionate lover is the natural enemy of temperance need not surprise us. For a young lady in love so to outrage Spenser's temperate man that he becomes intemperately passionate with "disdainefull wrath" need not surprise us either, if we are attuned to the humor of which the sage and serious Spenser is frequently capable.

The combat between Guyon and Britomart does not last for long. The palmer and Prince Arthur effect a truce, not by saying anything to Britomart—nor by assuring Guyon that, despite appearances to the contrary, she is actually a virtuous young lady—but simply by convincing the knight that his cause is hopeless:

For by his mightie Science he had seene
The secret vertue of that weapon keene,
That mortall puissance mote not withstond.
(III.i.10)

Britomart's secret power cannot at this point be identified with chastity, but can perhaps be interpreted as the mighty force of love, which overcomes all obstacles and to which reason and temperance must at least temporarily submit. The peace between Britomart and Guyon is still no

83

more than an uneasy détente. Not until the twelfth stanza, at the very end of this opening encounter, does Spenser first refer to chastity and tell us that permanent harmony has been reached.

> *Thus reconcilement was betweene them knit,*
> *Through goodly temperance, and affection chaste,*
> *And either vowd with all their power and wit,*
> *To let not others honour be defaste,*
> *Of friend or foe, who ever it embaste,*
> *Ne armes to beare against the others side:*
> *In which accord the Prince was also plaste,*
> *And with that golden chaine of concord tide.*
> *So goodly all agreed, they forth yfere did ride.*
>
> *(III.i.12)*

In a sense, this stanza and the incident it concludes form a prologue to the whole of Book III, a brief dumb show introducing the major theme to be developed, the reconciliation of temperance and passionate love in the chaste affection of marriage.[3] At the very start of Book III, then, Spenser has put his finger upon the central contradiction in contemporary attitudes toward love, the conflict between the romantic celebration of passion and the humanist emphasis on reason and temperance, and, what is more, he has promised in the course of his story to resolve that conflict.

Frequently in *The Faerie Queene* an incident is elucidated not so much by what precedes it in the narrative as by what immediately follows it. Spenser appears to delight in provoking our interest by

---

[3] This use of the opening incident to forecast the pattern of the entire book is not the only one in Spenser: the opening incident of Book I functions in precisely the same manner. See Hamilton, *Structure of Allegory,* pp. 40–43.

creating intellectual suspense. Thus he first presents us with the remarkable encounter between Guyon and the stranger, and only after the familiar champion has been thrown does he reveal who the other knight is. Further, it is not in the encounter with Guyon but in the adventures at Castle Joyous, the home of infidelity and excess, that he begins to define the precise nature of Britomart's passion and to suggest how the ultimate reconciliation between love and temperance is possible.

Just before he introduces us to Castle Joyous, Spenser gives us, by way of contrast to the adventures to come, a brief sketch of Britomart's constancy in her quest for Artegall. The lady knight is traveling in company with Arthur and Guyon when suddenly the beautiful Florimell rushes by in distress. The two knights, less interested in the lady's plight than in her beauty, immediately depart in pursuit. But such sport is not for Spenser's heroine:

> The whiles faire Britomart, whose constant mind,
>   Would not so lightly follow beauties chace,
>   Ne reckt of Ladies Love, did stay behind,
>   And them awaited there a certaine space,
>   To weet if they would turne backe to that place:
>   But when she saw them gone, she forward went,
>   As lay her journey, through that perlous Pace,
>   With stedfast courage and stout hardiment;
> Ne evill thing she fear'd, ne evill thing she ment.
>   (III.i.19)

The poet's touch is light—naturally Britomart is unmoved by feminine charms—but it is also sure: with an easy grace he has alerted us to the lady's faithfulness, her constant mind, the quality about to be tested at the House of Malecasta.

HEROIC LOVE

Britomart arrives at Castle Joyous to find six knights battling a solitary traveler in an attempt to compel him to renounce his lady.[4] As one of the six explains, their mistress has proclaimed a law

> *That every knight, which doth this way repaire,*
> *In case he have no Ladie, nor no love,*
> *Shall doe unto her service never to remove.*
>
> *But if he have a Ladie or a Love,*
> *Then must he her forgoe with foule defame,*
> *Or else with us by dint of sword approve,*
> *That she is fairer, then our fairest Dame,*
> *As did this knight, before ye hither came.*
> *Perdie (said Britomart) the choise is hard:*
> *But what reward had he, that overcame?*
> *He should advanced be to high regard,*
> *(Said they) and have our Ladies love for his reward.*
>   *(III.i.26–27)*

This "heads I win, tails you lose" proposition, another light touch, establishes a central fact about Castle Joyous: one way or another, change of love will be demanded of the visitor to the house of infidelity.

[4] This single knight, who is to be Britomart's companion throughout her stay at the castle, later turns out to be Redcross, but there is good reason to believe that at one time Spenser intended him to be Guyon. He once mistakenly calls the knight Guyon instead of Redcross, and he refers to him as a Fairy, a satisfactory epithet for Guyon who is a native of Fairyland but not for Redcross, a Briton. See Fredson Bowers, "Evidences of Revision in *The Faerie Queene* III.i,ii," *Modern Language Notes*, LX (1945), 114–116. Bowers believes that the substitution of Redcross for Guyon was made principally for the sake of the political allegory. Certainly Guyon would be a more appropriate companion in the moral allegory, for Malecasta's house is an offense to temperance but not specifically an offense to holiness. If it was indeed Spenser's original intention that the knight should be Guyon, then the companionship of Guyon and Britomart would have made it even more apparent that the poet is here beginning to develop the logic behind the reconciliation of the two.

Britomart easily defeats the six knights, but she still must contend with their mistress, she of the rolling eyes and fickle heart. The amorous approaches of this lady are of course no more serious a threat than Florimell's beauty, and for the most part Britomart simply pretends not to understand. Malecasta, however, is Lady Delight as well as Queen Inconstancy, and her house is suitably sumptuous. The material luxury of the palace—"Exceeding much the state of meane degree" (III.i.33), says Spenser—would appall Sir Guyon. The castle's luxury is in fact a concrete projection of the kind of love practiced there, a passion voluptuous and sensual to excess, and is as much a threat to Britomart as it is to Guyon. Its quality is suggested by the famous tapestry of Venus and Adonis adorning Malecasta's inner room, which, according to C. S. Lewis, presents a "picture not of 'lust in action' but of lust suspended—lust turning into what would now be called *skeptophilia*," a picture of perverted sexuality similar to that of the Bower of Bliss, where "there is not a kiss or an embrace in the island: only male prurience and female provocation." [5] It has been pointed out that in fact there are kisses and embraces in the bower, and that Lewis' interpretation depends upon an essentially modern assumption about the goodness of unsophisticated and unhindered sexuality, which becomes a misleading anachronism when applied to Spenser. "Skeptophilia" is not perhaps a wholly accurate term to describe the passion in the tapestry either, for we are told that Venus, having stolen Adonis' heart away, "joyed his love." But Lewis is quite right to emphasize the general absence of activity in the tapestry. Venus' love removes Adonis "from bright heavens vew," lulling him to sleep with gentle persuasion and substituting for the true heaven the painted simulacrum of her

---

[5] *Allegory of Love*, p. 332. For the criticism of Lewis, see N. S. Brooke, "C. S. Lewis and Spenser: Nature, Art and the Bower of Bliss," *Cambridge Journal*, II (1949), 420–434.

mantle, "colour'd like the starry skies," with which she covers the somnolent youth. This is no noble and daring love, but a slothful, timid passion. "Dreadfull of daunger, that mote him betide," the goddess attempts to keep her beloved boy from the hunt, attempts to keep him, that is, from an active life of honor. Such timidity is, to Spenser's mind, base. It is also futile, as he points out by reminding us that no one "can shun the chaunce, that dest'ny doth ordaine" (III.i.35–37). Despite everything Venus can do, Adonis is slain, and the pitiful fruit of their passion is but the dainty flower into which the youth is transformed.

Venus' timidity and sloth draw attention by contrast to Britomart's dedication to a noble, active life in her quest for Artegall. True love is to Spenser the opposite of sloth, "for love does alwayes bring forth bounteous deeds" (III.i.49); but the love to which Castle Joyous is given is remarkably sterile. Attempting to convert her to this luxurious life, Malecasta entreats Britomart to disarm: naturally her plea is in vain. Superficially, Malecasta and Britomart, passionate ladies both, have much in common. When Malecasta sees her guest's beauty and bursts into an "extreme desire," Britomart is convinced the lady genuinely loves her:

> *Full easie was for her to have beliefe,*
> *Who by self-feeling of her feeble sexe,*
> *And by long triall of the inward griefe,*
> *Wherewith imperious love her hart did vexe,*
> *Could judge what paines do loving harts perplexe.*
> *(III.i.54)*

Still Malecasta's desire, leading only to easeful sensuality, is no more than a "fine forgerie" of Britomart's own inward fire. Merely to have conceived a passion does not prove that one is either lecherous or virtuous. Rather that passion is a trial of the quality of the soul, and it is by what the passion achieves that the spirit will be revealed as noble or base.

> *Wonder it is to see, in diverse minds,*
>> *How diversly love doth his pageants play,*
>> *And shewes his powre in variable kinds:*
>> *The baser wit, whose idle thoughts alway*
>> *Are wont to cleave unto the lowly clay,*
>> *It stirreth up to sensuall desire,*
>> *And in lewd slouth to wast his carelesse day:*
>> *But in brave sprite it kindles goodly fire,*
> *That to all high desert and honour doth aspire.*
>
> *(III.v.1)*

But trial involves danger, and the lover's state is indeed a dangerous one. We recall Bembo's statement concerning the middle condition of human love, "where it is not safe to remain, for on a slope it is easier to slide into the depths than to clamber to the summit."

It is at Castle Joyous that Spenser gives us the first of his memorable descriptions of Britomart revealing her face to the world. Usually she is compared to the sun, but here the poet invokes chaste Diana, the moon:

> *As when faire Cynthia, in darkesome night,*
>> *Is in a noious cloud enveloped,*
>> *Where she may find the substaunce thin and light,*
>> *Breakes forth her silver beames, and her bright hed*
>> *Discovers to the world discomfited;*
>> *Of the poore traveller, that went astray,*

HEROIC LOVE

With thousand blessings she is heried;
Such was the beautie and the shining ray,
With which faire Britomart gave light unto the day.[6]

In the image of the moon in the "noious cloud," Spenser has captured perfectly the essence of Britomart's situation at this house of sloth and faithlessness. At Castle Joyous, Britomart has survived her first trial, has met and overcome the first dangers of her quest. Like the moon she emerges from the castle with a beauty more intense for the contrast with the cloud in which she has been enveloped. She emerges with a passion that has been proved noble. Britomart has not yet attained the summit of love, but she has shown herself unlikely to slide into the depths.

Spenser's heroine does not escape from Castle Joyous completely unscathed, however. Before she departs, she is struck by the keen arrow of Gardante. In a particularly vivid passage, Spenser describes how the lady's white smock becomes stained with red:

> *The mortall steele stayd not, till it was seene*
> *To gore her side, yet was the wound not deepe,*
> *But lightly rased her soft silken skin,*
> *That drops of purple bloud thereout did weepe,*
> *Which did her lilly smock with staines of vermeil steepe.*
> *(III.i.65)*

Britomart's assailant is one of the six knights who challenge all travelers to the castle, and the names of these knights are a more or less con-

---

[6] III.i.43. According to Dodge (*Var.* III, 210), this passage probably derives from the description of Bradamante disarming in *Orlando furioso*, XXXII.79–80. Ariosto's image is of the sun breaking from the clouds. Spenser's alteration of the image to the more significant one of the moon is an example of his creative use of sources.

90

ventional list of the stages of lecherous love from inception to culmination.[7]

> *The first of them by name Gardante hight,*
> *A jolly person, and of comely vew;*
> *The second was Parlante, a bold knight,*
> *And next to him Jocante did ensew;*
> *Basciante did him selfe most curteous shew;*
> *But fierce Bacchante seemd too fell and keene;*
> *And yet in armes Noctante greater grew:*
> *All were faire knights, and goodly well beseene,*
> *But to faire Britomart they all but shadowes beene.*
> *(III.i.45)*

The six steps on this ladder may be translated as seeing, speaking, toying, kissing, reveling, and copulating—personifications of the kind of activities to which Castle Joyous is devoted. The wound and resulting stain are clearly a reflection of some weakness in Britomart's character, but critics do not agree on precisely what this weakness is.[8]

[7] See Allan H. Gilbert, "The Ladder of Lechery, *The Faerie Queene*, III,i,45," *Modern Language Notes,* LVI (1941), 594–597; James Hutton, "Spenser and the 'Cinq Points en Amours,' " *Modern Language Notes,* LVII (1942), 657–661; and Alastair Fowler, "Six Knights at Castle Joyous," *Studies in Philology,* LVI (1959), 583–599.

[8] Gilbert, for example, suggests that the wound "perhaps signifies by allegory that only the first stage of lasciviousness can affect chastity, and that only to rouse resistance" ("The Ladder of Lechery," p. 594, n. 1). William Nelson thinks it indicates Britomart's "vulnerability to 'faire semblaunce,' "—*The Poetry of Edmund Spenser: A Study* (New York: Columbia University Press, 1963), p. 232. Roche, who discusses the matter at some length, believes the wound has a double meaning. It is, in the first place, Britomart's "initiation into the realities of love," for it compels her to recognize that love is more than an "interior passion," that it involves others, and that she herself is a possible "love object." In the second place, the wound represents the "everpresent dangers of maintaining chastity unimpaired in the active life. Britomart has merely 'countenanced' the

HEROIC LOVE

Most regard the wound as being a symbolic recapitulation of all that has happened at Malecasta's house, which I believe is looking for the significance in the wrong place. It seems to me that Spenser is here once again concluding an episode with an incident that is not elucidated until the following episode.

Britomart's wound comes at the end of the first canto of Book III. The second canto relates how the lady knight originally fell in love with Artegall, an event in her history that predates both her encounter with Guyon and her arrival at Castle Joyous. Just as Redcross' presence at Lucifera's castle is explicable only in terms of his earlier separation from Una, so Britomart's presence at Malecasta's house is explicable only in terms of her earlier experience, the momentous vision of Artegall in her father's magic mirror, the event that initiates her passion, her quest, and her story. The manner in which the poet has arranged this scene, having his heroine first view her beloved in the mirror, emphasizes the traditional notion of the inception of love through the eyes, and the language in which the scene is presented directs our attention to the same point. Spenser tells us that the image of the noble knight was "presented to her eye" (III.ii.24), and we are meant to understand that, falling in love, Britomart has been assaulted by Gardante, or Seeing. Love's weapon, like Gardante's, is the bow, and the immediate effect of Britomart's vision is a wound.

> But the false Archer, which that arrow shot
> So slyly, that she did not feele the wound,
> Did smile full smoothly at her weetlesse wofull stound.
> (III.ii.26)

world of unchastity, but this nevertheless puts her temporarily in the power of Gardante" (*Kindly Flame*, p. 70). For suggestions of a view anticipating my own, see Fowler, "Six Knights," pp. 598–599, and Hamilton, *Structure of Allegory*, p. 143.

92

Britomart's wound from Gardante's arrow is not a recapitulation of experiences at Castle Joyous, but a reference to that injury received from Cupid at the moment she saw Artegall in the mirror. Gardante, in fact, is an allegorical projection of Cupid in one of his aspects. Britomart's weakness is that she is a lover, and the stain on her smock represents her own passion, which has removed her from the number of the wholly temperate.

In being struck by Cupid's arrow Britomart has taken the first step onto the ladder of lechery and consequently must contend with the inhabitants of Castle Joyous. Yet seeing is the first rung on more ladders than that of lechery. An interesting analogue to the ladder formed by Malecasta's knights occurs in *As You Like It,* where Rosalind speaks of Orlando's brother and her sister as making a "pair of stairs to marriage." [9]

Your brother and my sister no sooner met but they look'd; no sooner look'd but they lov'd; no sooner lov'd but they sigh'd; no sooner sigh'd but they ask'd one another the reason; no sooner knew the reason but they sought the remedy—and in these degrees have they made a pair of stairs to marriage.   (V.ii.32–36)

Rosalind's ladder, not Malecasta's, is of course the one Britomart actually will climb, but Spenser's presentation of Castle Joyous indicates that another and less virtuous life might also have been hers.

Spenser evidently believed that a treatment of how Britomart fell in love was essential to his purposes, for he took the trouble to invent an episode not found in Ariosto. In the *Orlando furioso* Ariosto merely

[9] The analogue is noted by Hutton, "Spenser and the 'Cinq Points en Amours,'" p. 659.

declares that Bradamante is in love with Ruggiero, whom she has seen but once. Spenser fastened onto the fact that the heroine had only once seen her lover, and from this hint created out of the common materials of romance the story of Britomart's vision in the magic mirror. For the conversation between Britomart and Glauce, her nurse, he drew upon a similar scene in the pseudo-Vergilian *Ciris,* perhaps taking a few hints also from Ovid's tale of Myrrha. The story of the *Ciris* concerns the violent passion of Scylla for her father's enemy Minos, a passion that results in the girl's betrayal of her father and country and in death for herself. The *Ciris* is especially interesting as a source, for it was also in this epyllion that Spenser may have found the name Britomart, there a virgin huntress who meets death rather than lose her chastity to Minos. Spenser's Britomart, then, is a character created from a fusion of moral opposites, combining the attributes of the chaste virgin and the passionate Scylla.[10]

Britomart's novel ancestry does much to contribute to the ambivalence that marks her attitude toward her passion in its earliest stages. Her uncertainty about the value of her love is fully justified; at its inception her passion cannot be said to be worthy or unworthy, for it is untested. Britomart has fallen prey to the lover's malady, and she finds her illness repulsive, describing her condition in the language of disgust:

[10] On the relationship of this incident to Ariosto, see Dodge, *Var.* III, 370. There are many analogues to the magic mirror, but Spenser's source may well have been, as Warton proposed, the mirror in Chaucer's *Squire's Tale,* ll. 132–141 (see *Var.* III, 216–217). On the relation of the conversation with the nurse to the *Ciris* and Ovid, see Belden, *Var.* III, 219–220, and Hughes, *Var.* III, 334–337. The story of Britomartis was relatively familiar in classical times and in the Renaissance, and Spenser's particular source need not have been the *Ciris.* For a complete discussion of the matter, see John E. Hankins, "The Sources of Spenser's Britomartis," *Modern Language Notes,* LVIII (1943), 607–610. My discussion is indebted to Roche, *Kindly Flame,* pp. 53–55.

THE FAERIE QUEENE

all mine entrailes flow with poisnous gore,
And th'ulcer groweth daily more and more;
Ne can my running sore find remedie.
                                    (III.ii.39)

The stricken lady is unable to fight her passion but submits in despair, expecting to languish until her misery is ended by death. Utterly confused about whether her desire is wicked, she speaks of "my crime" and then immediately qualifies this with "if crime it be" (III.ii.37). Of only one thing is Britomart certain, that love's law is cruel and that she is in pain.

In her pain Britomart turns for help to her nurse, but Glauce is unable to resolve the girl's confusion. Britomart's nurse has frequently been interpreted as a character analogous to Guyon's palmer, that is, as a personified virtue, a moral guardian upon whom Britomart can rely.[11] But this is hardly the case. True heir of the long tradition shared by the old nurses in both the *Ciris* and Ovid's tale of Myrrha, Glauce is something of a bawd. The old lady is wise, but only in the ways of the world. Glauce knows life too well to be long puzzled by Britomart's symptoms. "Aye me," she cries, "how much I feare, least love it bee" (III.ii.33). The key to Glauce's character is that her allegiance is to Britomart herself rather than to any abstract notion of right or wrong. She advises her lady to conquer her passion, but if it cannot be suppressed then Britomart should be assured that she will do all in her power "by wrong or right / To compasse thy desire, and find that loved knight" (III.ii.46). Her single wish is that Britomart may be restored

[11] See, for example, W. F. DeMoss, who says that the nurse "in a measure represents Reason, or Prudence" (*Var.* III, 321), and Kathleen Williams, who believes Glauce provides for Britomart "a norm of health and sanity" in matters of love—*Spenser's "Faerie Queene": The World of Glass* (London: Routlege and Kegan Paul, 1966), p. 93.

to happiness: to that end she engages in a certain amount of sophistry in attempting to reconcile the young lady to her passion and, this failing, dabbles in charms to see if she can exorcise the passion completely. Glauce's experiment in magic is chronologically the earliest test of the fidelity of Britomart's passion, and it is at this point that Spenser, hitherto indulgent toward the old nurse, suggests his disapproval of Glauce's practices:

> *She turned her contrarie to the Sunne,*
> *Thrise she her turnd contrary, and returnd,*
> *All contrary, for she the right did shunne,*
> *And ever what she did, was streight undonne.*
> *So thought she to undoe her daughters love:*
> *But love, that is in gentle brest begonne,*
> *No idle charmes so lightly may remove,*
> *That well can witnesse, who by triall it does prove.*
> *(III.ii.51)*

Well may Spenser feel impatient with Glauce, for the herbs that the nurse is using in her charms—rue, savine, champhire, calamint, and dill—were said to produce barrenness as well as to abate the desires of venery.[12]

The third canto of Book III continues the story of Britomart's early experiences in love, telling how she and Glauce visited the cave of Merlin. In this episode, modeled upon Bradamante's visit to the tomb of Merlin in the *Orlando*, Spenser begins to resolve the moral ambiguity of the preceding canto, revealing by prophecy what the fruit of Britomart's passion is to be. The canto begins in a higher style than any we

---

[12] See Upton, *Var.* III, 221.

have yet seen in Book III. The portentous opening stanzas summarize
the themes to follow:

Most sacred fire, that burnest mightily
  In living brests, ykindled first above,
  Emongst th'eternall spheres and lamping sky,
  And thence pourd into men, which men call Love;
  Not that same, which doth base affections move
  In brutish minds, and filthy lust inflame,
  But that sweet fit, that doth true beautie love,
  And choseth vertue for his dearest Dame,
Whence spring all noble deeds and never dying fame:

Well did Antiquitie a God thee deeme,
  That over mortall minds hast so great might,
  To order them, as best to thee doth seeme,
  And all their actions to direct aright;
  The fatall purpose of divine foresight,
  Thou doest effect in destined descents,
  Through deepe impression of thy secret might,
  And stirredst up th'Heroes high intents,
Which the late world admires for wondrous moniments.

But thy dread darts in none doe triumph more,
  Ne braver proofe in any, of thy powre
  Shew'dst thou, then in this royall Maid of yore,
  Making her seeke an unknowne Paramoure,
  From the worlds end, through many a bitter stowre:
  From whose two loines thou afterwards did raise
  Most famous fruits of matrimoniall bowre,
  Which through the earth have spred their living praise,
That fame in trompe of gold eternally displayes.

(III.iii.1–3)

97

HEROIC LOVE

In the incident that follows this majestic prelude, the visit to the cave, everything is arranged to appear as impressive as possible. Ariosto's Bradamante is informed of her descendants not by Merlin but by an intermediary, Melissa. Spenser does away with the intermediary and gives us the "dreadfull Mage" himself. The reason for this careful pomp and circumstance is that Spenser is about to associate Britomart's story with the epic of British history and by this association to elevate her passion to a grandeur worthy of the highest vein of heroic poetry.

The substance of the canto is Merlin's prophecy of the names and deeds of the royal line to come from the union of Britomart and Artegall.

> *Renowmed kings, and sacred Emperours,*
> *Thy fruitfull Ofspring, shall from thee descend,*
> *Brave Captaines, and most mighty warriours,*
> *That shall their conquests through all lands extend,*
> *And their decayed kingdomes shall amend.*
>
> *(III.iii.23)*

Merlin traces the ancient British line down to Cadwallader and then rapidly surveys English history until the restoration of the British line in the Tudors. Gradually it becomes apparent that Britomart's true glory will be not that of a virago but of a mother. Her real achievement will be her "famous Progenie," for their valor will be her own splendor, and her "never dying fame" will rest ultimately on the fact that she has borne them. Spenser has reinterpreted the heroic ideals of the Middle Ages in terms of the Protestant attitude toward matrimony. The fidelity demanded of every medieval lover has become in his hands the fidelity demanded of a fiancé; the noble deeds in which true love was expected to flower have become the natural deed of wedlock, magnified to heroic proportions in the "famous fruits of matrimoniall bowre." The episode is in some ways a celebration of fecundity, analogous perhaps to the Garden of Adonis. But in the garden Spenser celebrates merely the generation of all natural creatures, whereas Merlin's prophecy is a chronicle of the generation of heroic spirits. It is a chronicle that cannot but remind us by contrast of the barren passions of Malecasta and Venus in Castle Joyous.

The history of Britomart's progeny is part of that providential plan the Elizabethans saw in their country's past, a grand scheme culminating in the union of Briton and Saxon, Lancastrian and Yorkist, in the royal house of Tudor. In the persons of the Tudors "shall the Briton bloud their crowne againe reclame."

> *Thenceforth eternall union shall be made*
> *Betweene the nations different afore,*
> *And sacred Peace shall lovingly perswade*
> *The warlike minds, to learne her goodly lore,*
> *And civile armes to exercise no more:*
> *Then shall a royall virgin raine, which shall*
> *Stretch her white rod over the Belgicke shore,*
> *And the great Castle smite so sore with all,*
> *That it shall make him shake, and shortly learne to fall.*
> *(III.iii.48–49)*

Thus even the great Queen Elizabeth, that "royall virgin," is a descendant of Britomart and Artegall. Britomart herself becomes a type of the Tudor Apocalypse when she puts on the armor of a Saxon queen named, significantly, Angela, thereby suggesting the union of both Angles and Saxons with the British line. It is clear now that Britomart's passion for Artegall is not the work of chance. In a passage that once

again reminds us by contrast of Malecasta and Castle Joyous, Merlin
reveals to the lady that it was not her "wandring eye,"

> *Glauncing unwares in charmed looking glas,*
> *But the streight course of heavenly destiny,*
> *Led with eternall providence, that has*
> *Guided thy glaunce, to bring his will to pas.*
> *(III.iii.24)*

Britomart's important role in the divine plan for England places an
enormous burden upon her. The conventional agonies of the passionate
lover are not mere psychological phenomena for her, but heroic trials
of the will to persevere: the entire future of England hangs upon the
success of her quest for Artegall. Significantly, it is not until after
Britomart has learned her high destiny from Merlin that she puts on
the armor of a champion. Before this she has been merely a lovesick
girl with a passion of dubious worth; now she is truly Britomartis,
Mars's Briton, determined to succeed.

Almost immediately after describing her donning of armor, Spenser
gives us an episode that chronologically should follow Britomart's stay
at Castle Joyous—it is more appropriately placed here, though, because
it tests and confirms her will to persevere. In the fifth stanza of canto
iv, he draws a brief sketch of the lady knight on her quest, constant in
her course, her mind fixed on her beloved. But as a result of thinking
so intently about Artegall,

> *her smart was much more grievous bred,*
> *And the deepe wound more deepe engord her hart,*
> *That nought but death her dolour mote depart.*
> *(III.iv.6)*

100

THE FAERIE QUEENE

Reaching the seashore, Britomart alights from her horse and partially disarms. Disarming and resting are usually ominous signs in Spenser, and so are they here, for Britomart is yielding to self-pity, fear, and despair:

> *Huge sea of sorrow, and tempestuous griefe,*
> *Wherein my feeble barke is tossed long,*
> *Far from the hoped haven of reliefe,*
> *Why do thy cruell billowes beat so strong,*
> *And thy moist mountaines each on others throng,*
> *Threatning to swallow up my fearfull life?*
> *O do thy cruell wrath and spightfull wrong*
> *At length allay, and stint thy stormy strife,*
> *Which in these troubled bowels raignes, and rageth rife.*

> *For else my feeble vessell crazd, and crackt*
> *Through thy strong buffets and outrageous blowes,*
> *Cannot endure, but needs it must be wrackt*
> *On the rough rocks, or on the sandy shallowes,*
> *The whiles that love it steres, and fortune rowes;*
> *Love my lewd Pilot hath a restlesse mind*
> *And fortune Boteswaine no assuraunce knowes,*
> *But saile withouten starres, gainst tide and wind:*
> *How can they other do, sith both are bold and blind?*
> $\qquad\qquad\qquad\qquad\qquad$ *(III.iv.8–9)*

Lamenting in the manner of a conventional Petrarchan lover, Britomart is rapidly sinking into a fearful sloth reminiscent of the Venus of the tapestry, when she is brought up short by Glauce, who reminds her of the glorious future Merlin prophesied. It is just at this moment that a knight appears on the horizon, galloping toward her in full armor. Pulling on her helmet, Britomart leaps to her horse, and after a dis-

101

dainful exchange of words the two knights charge at each other. At the first encounter the lady is almost defeated, but her moment of weakness passes, and in the second charge she strikes

With so fierce furie and great puissaunce,
That through his threesquare scuchin percing quite,
And through his mailed hauberque, by mischaunce
The wicked steele through his left side did glaunce;
Him so transfixed she before her bore
Beyond his croupe, the length of all her launce,
Till sadly soucing on the sandie shore,
He tombled on an heape, and wallowd in his gore.

(III.iv.16)

Once again Spenser explains an encounter only after it has occurred, revealing to us after Britomart's departure that the conquered knight was Marinell, one who had been trained from childhood to fear love. Britomart's conquest of Marinell after first coming close to defeat at his hands is emblematic of her conquest of her own fears after the moment of despair. In this important victory the full measure of her will and determination has been displayed, and her commitment to the quest for Artegall has been confirmed in heroic trial.

Having conquered Marinell, Britomart rides off on her quest and, although Spenser tells us that "fairely well she thriv'd, and well did brooke / Her noble deeds, ne her right course for ought forsooke" (III.iv.44), we shall not actually meet the lady knight again until the ninth canto of Book III, when she reappears at Malbecco's castle. At this point, midway through the fourth canto, a unified section of the epic has been completed, and Spenser turns his attention to other matters. There is relatively little further development of Britomart herself in *The Faerie Queene*.

The logic of the section through which we have traveled should now be clear. In these cantos we have witnessed the growth of Britomart from a young girl, as ignorant of herself as of the world around her, into a great lady of considerable wisdom and knowledge. Britomart began her career with such naiveté that she was even unaware that her malady was love, and at the cave of Merlin she had to discover, in a sense, who she was. Her introduction to the world at large came at Castle Joyous, where her ignorance of "malengine and fine forgerie" led to her misjudging of Malecasta's character. When she left the castle, Britomart's formal education was complete: all that remained to be tested was her determination not to yield to her own fears and doubts of success. Chronologically, then, Spenser has given us a consistent picture of Britomart's growth. But he has not chosen to tell his story in chronological order, and for good reason. All along, his chief interest has been not Britomart's development but the moral significance of her passion, and every incident in the narrative has been organized so as to create from this progressive revelation of moral significance an exciting and suspenseful story.

ARTEGALL IN LOVE

Artegall and Britomart first encounter one another at Satyrane's tournament, in Book IV. Unrecognized by Britomart because he is disguised as the Salvage Knight, Artegall's ferocious behavior, slashing shields and helmets, beating down whoever dares approach him, is echoed in his costume, which

> *was like salvage weed*
> *With woody mosse bedight, and all his steed*
> *With oaken leaves attrapt, that seemed fit*
> *For salvage wight, and thereto well agreed*
> *His word, which on his ragged shield was writ,*
> Salvagesse sans finesse, *shewing secret wit.*
>   *(IV.iv.39)*

The significance of the costume lies in Artegall's being "rebellious unto love," the passion that is the "crowne of knighthood" (IV.vi.31) and forms the distinction between *cortois* and *vilain*, and without which he is in fact a savage. Yet the savage costume is merely a disguise: the true Artegall is not this knight but the ideal man he will become once his "salvagesse" has been tempered by love. It is this Artegall of the future that Britomart viewed in her father's magic mirror.

> *A comely knight, all arm'd in complete wize,*
> *Through whose bright ventaile lifted up on hye*
> *His manly face, that did his foes agrize,*
> *And friends to termes of gentle truce entize,*
> *Lookt foorth, as Phoebus face out of the east,*
> *Betwixt two shadie mountaines doth arize;*
> *Portly his person was, and much increast*
> *Through his Heroicke grace, and honorable gest.*
>   *(III.ii.24)*

Having fallen in love with this ideal champion, it is hardly surprising that Britomart fails to recognize the Salvage Knight as her future husband.[1]

At the tournament Britomart unseats Artegall with her enchanted spear; but when next they meet, Artegall fights on foot and is beginning to get the better of his foe when an unexpected event occurs, revealing the lady's "angels face" and spelling defeat for the knight. Artegall is astonished at her beauty.

> *And he himselfe long gazing thereupon,*
> *At last fell humbly downe upon his knee,*
> *And of his wonder made religion,*
> *Weening some heavenly goddesse he did see,*
> *Or else unweeting, what it else might bee;*
> *And pardon her besought his errour fraile,*
> *That had done outrage in so high degree:*
> *Whilest trembling horrour did his sense assaile,*
> *And made ech member quake, and manly hart to quaile.*
>
> *(IV.vi.22)*

With conventional suddenness, the Salvage Knight has fallen in love. Shedding his disguise, he raises his beaver and reveals to Britomart "the lovely face of Artegall." No longer fierce and wild, his countenance now is "tempred with sternesse and stout majestie" (IV.vi.26). He has received the crown of knighthood and become recognizable as the champion of Britomart's vision.

But in ceasing to be a woman hater, Artegall has gone to the other extreme and become an idolator, turning his wonder into religion. Once disdainful of women, he now prostrates himself before Britomart

---

[1] On the significance of Artegall's disguise, see Roche, *Kindly Flame,* p. 89.

in a most unsuitable manner. Sir Scudamour is present and is amused to see his companion pass from one extreme to the other so rapidly.

> Certes Sir Artegall,
> I joy to see you lout so low on ground,
> And now become to live a Ladies thrall,
> That whilome in your minde wont to despise them all.
> (IV.vi.28)

"Wise Nature," says Spenser elsewhere, has subjected woman to man and bound the female sex "t'obay the heasts of mans well ruling hand" (V.v.25). By prostrating himself before a woman, Artegall has abdicated his proper role in the natural order of things, and this violation of natural order is for Spenser no less a form of injustice than if a monarch should submit to the rule of his subjects. Spenser's discussion of Artegall's susceptibility to this form of injustice is appropriately reserved for Book V, where it is treated in the story of his captivity by the Amazon Radigund.

The Amazon, as we have already seen in connection with the *Arcadia*, was a figure commonly associated with the injustice of female rule. Spenser's Radigund is just such a tyrant, a notable example of

> the crueltie of womenkind,
> When they have shaken off the shamefast band,
> With which wise Nature did them strongly bind.
> (V.v.25)

Radigund's custom is to conquer wayfaring knights, strip them of their arms, dress them in woman's clothes, and set them to the unseemly tasks of woman's work. Artegall has vowed to end her misdeeds, but the knight of justice, himself now subject to a woman, is ill suited to right this particular wrong. His fight with Radigund repeats almost exactly the pattern of his encounter with Britomart in the forest. Just as with Britomart, he is on the point of winning when suddenly his foe's helmet is opened and her face revealed. The Amazon's beauty overwhelms him; he drops his sword, declares himself defeated, and submits to her mercy.

> So was he overcome, not overcome,
>   But to her yeelded of his owne accord;
>   Yet was he justly damned by the doome
>   Of his owne mouth, that spake so wareless word,
>   To be her thrall, and service her afford.
>   (V.v.17)

Sir Scudamour's earlier comment is equally appropriate to Artegall's present defeat: the proud knight has now become a lady's thrall.

As a rebel against love, Artegall wore the disguise of the Salvage Knight; now, having gone to the opposite extreme, he is once more disguised, this time in woman's clothes as a sign of his effeminacy. Once again Britomart helps to restore her beloved to his true self, defeating Radigund, freeing her imprisoned men, and dressing Artegall in more dignified attire.

Just as Artegall's coming into Radigund's power is related to his earlier falling in love, so Britomart's freeing him from subjection is connected with the progress of the knight's courtship in Book IV. After falling to his knees at the sight of Britomart's face, Artegall begins to woo in proper courtly fashion, submitting himself to the mercy of his lady "with meeke service and much suit" (IV.vi.40). In the same courtly fashion Britomart responds, hiding her love—her "wound," as

Spenser puts it—and allowing Artegall to humble himself, since only gradually should a lady be won. As a result of her respect for decorum, Britomart has found herself temporarily in the role of the cruel lady, familiar to us from the sonnet sequences. The tyrannous lady of the sonnets never yields, for courtship in this tradition is an end in itself. But Britomart is no tyrant—hers is a "gentle hart"—and marriage rather than an eternity of courtship is her goal:

> So well he woo'd her, and so well he wrought her,
>   With faire entreatie and sweet blandishment,
>   That at the length unto a bay he brought her,
>   So as she to his speeches was content
>   To lend an eare, and softly to relent.
>   At last through many vowes which forth he pour'd,
>   And many othes, she yeelded her consent
>   To be his love, and take him for her Lord,
> Till they with marriage meet might finish that accord.
>   (IV.vi.41)

At one level, the Radigund episode is evidently a recapitulation of Artegall's courtship of Britomart. We must not be misled by the fact that Radigund herself is in love with Artegall. This is no more than the usual stuff of romance. In fact the Amazon is the cruel lady of the sonnet sequences, become an actual rather than a metaphorical tyrant.[2] The subjection in which she maintains her captive knights is no more than a concrete realization of the total subjection demanded by the convention of the wooing knight. Allegorically, Radigund is Britomart herself in her role as Artegall's mistress and lady. Britomart frees her lover from the iron prison of the Amazon by herself shedding the role

---

[2] For this point I am indebted to Caroline Collins Hunt.

of the proud lady, by relenting and taking Artegall "for her Lord." This restoration of the proper relationship between the sexes marks the end of courtship and the first stage in the commencement of married love.

The Radigund episode thus constitutes Spenser's criticism of the courtly conventions of the cruel lady and the pleading lover. Of course this is not to say that the poet desired any serious change in the conventions of courtship. Spenser would not conceive of such a matter in unconventional terms. He sees courtship not as wicked but as unjust. The difference between him and most of his predecessors is that for him, as for Britomart, courtship is no end in itself, but merely a means to the great goal of married love.

BUSYRANE AND MARRIED LOVE

According to C. S. Lewis' celebrated theory, *The Faerie Queene* recounts the story of a great struggle in which the opponents are courtly love and married love or chastity, a struggle in which courtly love is roundly defeated.

To find the real foe of Chastity, the real portrait of false love, we must turn to Malecasta and Busirane. The moment we do so, we find that Malecasta and Busirane are nothing else than the main subject of this study—Courtly Love; and that Courtly Love is in Spenser's view the chief opponent of Chastity. But Chastity for him means Britomart, married love. The story he tells is therefore part of my story: the final struggle between the romance of marriage and the romance of adultery.[1]

[1] *Allegory of Love*, p. 340.

109

Lewis' identification of false love with courtly love seems to me misleading. Spenser's own distinction between true love and false is no more radical than Chaucer's in *Troilus and Criseyde*: it is the distinction between fidelity and infidelity. As John Upton, one of the earliest editors of *The Faerie Queene*, put it in 1758, "affection and love to *one*, and only to *one*, is the chast affection which he holds up to your view, and to your imitation." [2] Again and again Spenser tests the quality of his characters' passions by subjecting them to trials of fidelity. Britomart is tried at Castle Joyous and Amoret at the House of Busyrane. Florimell's fidelity to Marinell proves more powerful even than the temptations and threats of a god, Proteus:

> Die had she rather in tormenting griefe,
> Then any should of falsenesse her reprove,
> Or loosenesse, that she lightly did remove.
>   (*III.viii.42*)

Of course fidelity is not in itself the source of virtue but merely a manifestation of the ultimate source, nobility of spirit, that mysterious quality as involuntary and predetermined for Spenser as salvation or damnation is to an orthodox Calvinist. Let one of Spenser's elect become impassioned, and he blazes with the glory of a faithful love that "to all high desert and honour doth aspire." Yet let the "baser wit" be wounded by Cupid, and he burns in lust and "in lewd slouth" wastes "his carelesse day" (III.v.1). C. S. Lewis' courtly lover—that is, the passionate lover of the troubadour tradition—was no enemy of Spenser's. As faithful to his own mistress as Britomart is to Artegall, the conventional courtly lover would have fought just as stoutly as she against those six knights at Malecasta's house of infidelity. Malecasta is indeed

2 *Var.* III, 310.

one of Spenser's portraits of false passion, but she is not to be identified with courtly love.

Lewis' identification of Britomart with chastity is also misleading, not only because it reduces her to a simple allegorical counter, but also because it imposes upon Spenser too limited a conception of this virtue. Chastity for Spenser embraces virginity as well as married love. The development of the Protestant attitude toward matrimony did not mean a complete rejection of the old ideal of virginity; instead there was a general elevation of the moral status of wedlock until the new ideal seemed the twin of the old. In *The Faerie Queene* these two forms of chastity, virginity and matrimony, are embodied in the twin sisters, Belphoebe and Amoret. As we saw earlier, the married state was so lauded by Protestants that it frequently came to seem the superior of virginity, but Spenser was in this, as in so many other matters, somewhat old-fashioned. Despite Luther and Calvin, he believed the clergy should remain celibate, and for him virginity still stood upon "the highest staire / Of th'honorable stage of womanhead" (III.v.54). Spenser might make virginity and married love twin sisters, but he was also careful to make Belphoebe the elder of the two.[3]

There is no struggle between married love and courtly love in *The Faerie Queene*. The story Spenser tells is of the proving of the faithful

[3] Belphoebe and Amoret's names imply definite allegorical functions in a way that Britomart's, suggesting a bold warrior rather than an abstract virtue, does not. It is clear from their miraculous birth and supernatural rearing by Diana and Venus, respectively, that the twins exist on an entirely different narrative level from Britomart. For an excellent critical discussion identifying the twins as virginity and married love, see Roche, *Kindly Flame*, pp. 96–146. I disagree, however, with Roche's further identification of the twins as the two Venuses of the Neoplatonists, on which see Ellrodt, *Neoplatonism in the Poetry of Spenser*, pp. 48–49. For Spenser's opinion on clerical celibacy, see Virgil K. Whitaker, *The Religious Basis of Spenser's Thought* (Stanford: Stanford University Press, 1950), pp. 18–19, and Ellrodt, p. 197. Spenser twice points out that Belphoebe is older than Amoret (III.vi.4 and III.vi.51).

passion of Britomart and Artegall, a love leading toward marriage. This passion is somewhat at odds with both temperance and justice, but its goal is noble, and in marriage a reconciliation with those virtues will be effected. Spenser's story is not, then, the struggle between two opposed forms of love, but rather the transformation of passionate love into matrimonial love. As I shall try to show, Britomart's victory over Busyrane describes not so much the rejection of a false form of love as the rejection of a now untimely passion, a passion that has served its purpose and is needed no longer.

The outlines of the Busyrane episode come from the second and fourth cantos of the *Orlando furioso*, where Ariosto recounts an adventure of a lamenting knight, a captive lady, a fiery castle, a dreadful enchanter, and the brave heroine, Bradamante, who triumphs over them all. In fact the beginning of the story as Spenser tells it, Britomart's discovery of Sir Scudamour weeping for his lost lady, is translated almost literally from the Italian incident in which Bradamante discovers a young knight seated, like Scudamour, by a fountain, lamenting that his mistress is imprisoned in Atlante's castle. The course of Ariosto's narrative is, in a general way, similar to Spenser's. Bradamante undertakes to free the lady from Atlante, which she does with the aid of a magic ring that has the power to expose falsehood. Upon her command, the enchanter extinguishes the fires, the weird castle vanishes, and the captives are freed.[4]

Ariosto's sixteenth-century commentators, perhaps not entirely against the poet's own intentions in this case, turned the story of Bradamante's

[4] On the Ariostan sources of the Busyrane episode, see Dodge, *Var.* III, 288, and McMurphy, *Var.* III, 372–373. A great many other influences have been traced. See esp. Blanchard, *Var.* III, 289–290; Koeppel, *Var.* III, 290–291; Greenlaw, *Var.* III, 359–366; and Dorothy F. Atkinson, "Busirane's Castle and Artidon's Cave," *Modern Language Quarterly*, I (1940), 185–192.

conquest of the enchanter into an allegory. Atlante's castle was understood to represent carnal desire, the key to this interpretation being its
protecting fires, obvious emblems of the ardors and sighs of passion.
The story as a whole was thought to signify the conquest of earthly
love (Atlante) by divine love (Bradamante) through the use of reason,
symbolized by the magic ring.[5] Without doubt this allegorical reading
of Ariosto influenced Spenser; yet this is not to say that the meaning of
his episode is identical with the Italian poet's. Busyrane's castle, like
Atlante's, is a house of earthly love. But in Book III of *The Faerie
Queene* earthly love forms the entire amatory spectrum: Malecasta,
Florimell, Britomart, Hellenore, Scudamour, Paridell, and Amoret,
diverse as their passions are, all are carnal lovers. In denying that
matrimony was a sacrament, the Protestant reformers removed human
love from the order of grace and established it firmly in the order of
nature, and for this reason divine love plays no part in Spenser's scheme
for Book III, just as it played no part in Sidney's scheme for the *Arcadia*. Ariosto's commentators were committed to the ideal of virginity,
but Spenser, a Protestant, has no wish to reject carnal love entirely;
his object is its perfection in matrimony, and with this his story of the
enchanted castle is concerned.

The knight that Britomart discovers weeping for his lady is a man
overwhelmed by passion. Hardly able to speak, Scudamour just manages to explain Amoret's plight when he is cut off by his own sobs. So
completely has he yielded to grief that he has begun to doubt divine
justice, questioning the worth of virtue "if goodnesse find no grace, nor
righteousnesse no meed" (III.xi.9). In contrast with Scudamour, Britomart is restrained and reasonable, and with a brief homily on submis-
sion to providence she advises against despair. Together they set off for

[5] See McMurphy, *Spenser's Use of Ariosto*, p. 34.

113

Amoret's prison, but at the sight of the fiery porch Scudamour is already willing to give up. Britomart is more judicious. She has no thought of admitting defeat so soon—it would be shameful "t'abandon noble chevisaunce, / For shew of perill, without venturing" (III.xi.24)—but neither does she underestimate the danger. In her opinion the taking of a fiery castle requires some serious ratiocination, some planning and consideration, for to attempt a danger without the application of reason to the problem would be "inglorious and beastlike."

Spenser emphasizes the contrast between the passionate man and the reasonable lady because it is precisely this difference that explains why Britomart alone is able to walk through the wall of fire. The lady covers her face with her shield, raises her sword, and passes easily through:

> *Whom whenas Scudamour saw past the fire,*
> *Safe and untoucht, he likewise gan assay,*
> *With greedy will, and envious desire,*
> *And bad the stubborne flames to yield him way:*
> *But cruell Mulciber would not obay*
> *His threatfull pride, but did the more augment*
> *His mighty rage, and with imperious sway*
> *Him forst (maulgre) his fiercenesse to relent,*
> *And backe retire, all scorcht and pitifully brent.*
> *(III.xi.26)*

These flames, like those of Atlante's castle, are the fires of passion, and in such a case a desperate charge to the fore is a tactical error. In the face of Scudamour's fury, naturally the fire waxes greater, and just as naturally it yields to the dispassionate Britomart. Like Bradamante before her, Britomart is conquering the enchanter's castle with the ring of reason.

114

THE FAERIE QUEENE

Once inside, the heroine discovers the tapestry of Cupid's wars, that vast panorama of the power of the blind god before whose idol all the people in Busyrane's house have gathered to worship. The tapestry, illustrating the irresistibility of passion, is described in imagery reminiscent of the wall of fire. We hear, for example, of Jove's "scalding smart" and of the "scorching heat" that Leda attempted to avoid. It is covered with tales of grief, distress, terror, and death, and the description concludes with an awful image of human confusion and general torment:

> *Kings Queenes, Lords Ladies, Knights and Damzels gent*
> *Were heap'd together with the vulgar sort,*
> *And mingled with the raskall rablement,*
> *Without respect of person or of port,*
> *To shew Dan Cupids powre and great effort:*
> *And round about a border was entraild,*
> *Of broken bowes and arrowes shivered short,*
> *And a long bloudy river through them raild,*
> *So lively and so like, that living sence it faild.*
>
> *(III.xi.46)*

Extreme passion, Spenser reminds us, is the great untuner of degree, the enemy of order and dignity, a force so powerful that it can transform even a god into a beast.

The tapestry emphasizes the pains and dangers of desire, but it is not necessary to suppose that the passions portrayed are all base, even though they are all frightening. Spenser's representation of lust, of the kind of voluptuous life led by the inhabitants of Castle Joyous, is not the tapestry but the golden chamber that Britomart enters next, and this is specifically contrasted with the hall of the tapestry.

115

HEROIC LOVE

Much fairer, then the former, was that roome,
And richlier by many partes arayd:
For not with arras made in painefull loome,
But with pure gold it all was overlaid,
Wrought with wilde Antickes, which their follies playd,
In the rich metall, as they living were:
A thousand monstrous formes therein were made,
Such as false love doth oft upon him weare,
For love in thousand monstrous formes doth oft appeare.
(III.xi.51)

The tapestry, too, has its gold, but false love makes up only one part of the fabric of Cupid's triumph, the more insidious, more dangerous part because it is the less apparent. The cloth is

Woven with gold and silke so close and nere,
That the rich metall lurked privily,
As faining to be hid from envious eye;
Yet here, and there, and every where unwares
It shewd it selfe, and shone unwillingly;
Like a discolourd Snake, whose hidden snares
Through the greene gras his long bright burnisht backe declares.
(III.xi.28)

In the light of the golden chamber, the meaning of these lurking metal strands is obvious. But what does Spenser mean by the more frank and open silk threads, clearly of a different order from the gold? Probably they represent faithful passion, which, true as it is, still stands so near to lust that only time, as Britomart's case has shown, can finally distinguish one from the other.

116

That the tapestry presents so distressing a vision of even faithful passion need not surprise us, unless we are misled by our own romantic preference for the ecstasies of courtship over the quiet affection of marriage. Spenser, for whom courtship is an experience always more sour than sweet, never regards the passionate lover with modern sentimentality. Too often we forget that Britomart's vision in her father's mirror introduces her to suffering rather than joy. Driven almost to distraction by the disease festering within her, annoyed by the inhabitants of Castle Joyous, forced dangerously close to despair, the single delight Britomart ever finds in passion is the assured knowledge given her by Merlin that some day her pains will cease and she will be united with Artegall in a more pleasurable form of affection. Spenser compares the course of her love to a plant,

> *Whose root and stalke so bitter yet did tast,*
> *That but the fruit more sweetnesse did containe,*
> *Her wretched dayes in dolour she mote wast,*
> *And yield the pray of love to lothsome death at last.*
> *(III.ii.17)*

The sweet fruit is temperate married love, which grows upon the bitter root and stalk of passionate desire. Spenser values the plant for its fruit, not its bitter stem. Yet without the stem there would be no fruit. Passion, the power Busyrane represents, is not intrinsically evil. In a Malecasta it will be debased into lust, but by the same power a Britomart or an Amoret will be spurred to marriage. Before the joys of temperate marital affection can be realized, however, intemperate passion with all its attendant pains must be banished; the lover must become reasonable again—or, as Spenser puts it, he must be freed from the House of Busyrane.

The usual interpretation of the Busyrane episode is that the enchanter represents a form of lust to which Amoret is susceptible, a result of her training in the Garden of Adonis. Brought up in the fecund garden, Amoret cannot refrain from surrendering herself to extreme sensuality under the sanction of marriage. She is unprepared to understand the spiritual values of matrimony.[6] Amoret's education is more adequate than this interpretation would suggest, for actually she is educated in not one but two schools, the Garden of Adonis and the Temple of Venus, schools that together provide her with a thorough preparation for a life of married love.

The Garden of Adonis has probably been the subject of more critical discussion than any passage in Spenser, and I do not propose to fathom its depths. Fortunately, however, recent criticism appears to be arriving at some kind of agreement upon certain basic facts.[7] Most scholars now

[6] For this view, see Padelford, *Var.* III, 326, and see also Donald Cheney, *Spenser's Image of Nature: Wild Man and Shepherd in "The Faerie Queene"* (New Haven: Yale University Press, 1966), p. 138, and Williams, *Spenser's "Faerie Queene,"* p. 105. For a very different view of the House of Busyrane, see Roche, *Kindly Flame,* pp. 72–88, to whom I am especially indebted in my discussion of the Masque of Cupid. Roche's interpretation is so complex that I cannot attempt to summarize it adequately, but in general it may be said that he believes the House of Busyrane to be an objectification of Amoret's fears of marriage.

[7] Charles G. Osgood provides a convenient summary of early discussions of the garden (*Var.* III, 340–352), including Josephine Waters Bennett's well-known "Spenser's Garden of Adonis," *PMLA,,* XLVII (1932), 46–80, and Brents Stirling's "The Philosophy of Spenser's Garden of Adonis," *PMLA, XLIX* (1934), 501–538. Mrs. Bennett is the defender of the Neoplatonic interpretation, while Stirling argues that Spenser is merely using Renaissance commonplaces. See also Mrs. Bennett's "Spenser's Garden of Adonis Revisited," *Journal of English and Germanic Philology,* XLI (1942), 53–78; Stirling's response, "Spenser's

seem to think that the garden embodies no all-embracing cosmological system: Spenser is not giving us his complete picture of the universe, but merely his portrait of the constant renewal of the physical life of the world. We read that the garden is the meeting place of form and substance, but these puzzling terms are now thought to refer more to popular ideas of shape and matter than to the subtle abstractions of the Platonists or Aristotelians. Spenser tells us that the creatures in the garden possess no souls—they are mere "shapes," although some, the ones destined to become human beings, are shapes "fit for reasonable soules t'indew" (III.vi.35). Not even the developing human shapes have souls: this suggests that the garden is located in the order of nature rather than grace, and confirms the usual impression of readers that Spenser's teeming garden is a great celebration of sexual genera-tion. In this garden Amoret is trained in "goodly womanhed"—that is, in the purely natural, purely physical aspects of her future role as wife and mother. What she obtains here is the science every female creature, animal as well as human, requires: the knowledge of reproduction.

In the Temple of Venus her education is carried beyond the natural as she is trained in the virtues that will suit her for a life as a reasonable creature. The key difference between the garden and the temple is

---

'Platonic' Garden," *Journal of English and Germanic Philology*, XLI (1942), 482–486; and her "Reply: On Methods of Literary Interpretation," *Journal of English and Germanic Philology*, XLI (1942), 486–489. Whatever consensus does exist appears to be based more or less upon Stirling's point of view. For exam-ples of recent criticism, see esp. Ellrodt, *Neoplatonism in the Poetry of Spenser*, pp. 70–90; C. S. Lewis' review of Ellrodt in *Etudes anglaises*, XIV (1961), 107–116; Hough, *Preface to "The Faerie Queene,"* pp. 176–179; Nelson, *Poetry of Edmund Spenser*, pp. 207–223; Roche, *Kindly Flame*, pp. 117–128; Cheney, *Spenser's Image of Nature*, pp. 117–145; A. Bartlett Giamatti, *The Earthly Para-dise and the Renaissance Epic* (Princeton: Princeton University Press, 1966), pp. 284–290; and Williams, *Spenser's "Faerie Queene,"* pp. 103–105, 145–150.

that, where the garden demonstrates the best that unaided nature can produce, in the temple nature has been perfected by human art.[8] The garden is "so faire a place, as Nature can devize" (III.vi.29). The temple is superior:

> *For all that nature by her mother wit*
> *Could frame in earth, and forme of substance base,*
> *Was there, and all that nature did omit,*
> *Arte playing second natures part, supplied it.*
>
> *(IV.x.21)*

We should notice the contrasts between the garden and the temple. The seedbeds of the garden, swarming with life, have their opposite in the temple's manicured lawns, where the multitudes of true lovers and friends take their decorous pleasures among the even ranks of trees. The central feature of the garden, the Mount of Venus—Spenser's allusion is anatomical—contrasts with the temple itself, famous for its "goodly workmanship," a sanctum produced by art rather than nature. The arbor of Venus and Adonis in the mount's "thickest covert"

---

[8] In C. S. Lewis' view, Spenser regarded art as the corrupter of nature (*Allegory of Love*, pp. 329–330), but this has been shown to be erroneous. Spenser, like most of his contemporaries, probably regarded art as the perfecter of a nature which, being fallen, cannot perfect itself. Only when art sets itself up as nature's competitor, as the creator of a false nature like the Bower of Bliss, does Spenser disapprove, for then art has become nature's enemy and the harmony of the cosmos has been disturbed. See Brooke, "C. S. Lewis and Spenser: Nature, Art and the Bower of Bliss," pp. 420–434; Miller MacLure, "Nature and Art in *The Faerie Queene*," *ELH*, XXVIII (1961), 1–20, who discusses the correspondences between the garden and the temple; and Hans P. Guth, "Allegorical Implications of Artifice in Spenser's *Faerie Queene*," *PMLA*, LXXVI (1961), 474–479.

contrasts with the "inmost Temple," containing the altar and idol of Venus. In this very civilized place, this sanctum sanctorum of civilization, Amoret is found, seated in the lap of Womanhood, who personifies what she earlier learned in the Garden of Adonis. Surrounding her are a series of new figures, personifications of the virtues she has learned here, the qualities with which human reason has perfected nature: Shamefastness, Cheerfulness, Modesty, Courtesy, Silence, and Obedience. Far from being inadequate, Amoret's education is precisely of the kind that would have restrained her from surrendering to mere natural impulse in marriage. It is not a Christian education—recall that Spenser did not regard matrimony as an exclusively Christian state—but for her limited role, Amoret's training will suffice.

The Busyrane episode picks up Amoret's story at the moment her married life is about to begin. As we learn in Book IV, Busyrane's capture of the lady has occurred between the wedding feast and the bedding of the bride. The general impression that the House of Busyrane leaves on the reader is very different from that left by Spenser's real house of lust, Castle Joyous: there the impression is of decadent voluptuousness, of flaccid, bored sensuality, of things stagnant and rotting; but here the overriding sense is one of nightmarish frustration, of something striving and yet powerless to be born. Amoret is imprisoned in her tormenting passion for Scudamour: she yearns to be free, to enter upon the happy and fruitful life that is her destiny, but does not know how to escape.

Amoret's prison is the world of the Petrarchan sonnets come to life. The sonneteer compares his desire to a consuming flame, and thus Busyrane's castle is literally surrounded by fire. The lover complains of the storm of his sighs and tears, and thus Spenser tells how when night fell

121

HEROIC LOVE

an hideous storme of winde arose,
With dreadfull thunder and lightning atwixt,
And an earth-quake, as if it streight would lose
The worlds foundations from his centre fixt.
(III.xii.2)

Love is compared to a wound from Cupid's arrow, and thus Amoret's heart is transfixed with a "deadly dart." The lover is said to wear Venus' chains, and thus she is chained to a brass pillar. Love is spoken of as an enchanter, and thus Spenser gives us a real enchanter, Busyrane.

Day after day, with no end in sight, Amoret must take part in the Masque of Cupid, the parade of passions in which she is trapped. The figures in this masque march in an order roughly corresponding to the progress of a love affair, beginning with the prologue Ease, for by long tradition love was understood to require leisure. Next comes Fancy, the lover's idle imagination, which gives birth to Desire, followed by Doubt, Danger, Fear, Hope, Dissemblance, Suspect, Grief, Fury, Displeasure, and Pleasance.

After all these there marcht a most faire Dame,
Led of two grysie villeins, th'one Despight,
The other cleped Cruelty by name:
She dolefull Lady, like a dreary Spright,
Cald by strong charmes out of eternall night,
Had deathes owne image figurd in her face,
Full of sad signes, fearefull to living sight;
Yet in that horror shewd a seemely grace,
And with her feeble feet did move a comely pace.

Her brest all naked, as net ivory,
    Without adorne of gold or silver bright,
    Wherewith the Craftesman wonts it beautify,
    Of her dew honour was despoiled quight,
    And a wide wound therein (O ruefull sight)
    Entrenched deepe with knife accursed keene,
    Yet freshly bleeding forth her fainting spright,
    (The worke of cruell hand) was to be seene,
That dyde in sanguine red her skin all snowy cleene.

At that wide orifice her trembling hart
    Was drawn forth, and in silver basin laid,
    Quite through transfixed with a deadly dart,
    And in her bloud yet steeming fresh embayd:
    And those two villeins, which her steps upstayd,
    When her weake feete could scarcely her sustaine,
    And fading vitall powers gan to fade,
    Her forward still with torture did constraine,
And evermore encreased her consuming paine.
                                        (III.xii.19–21)

Melancholy, pale, and close to death, Amoret is a textbook case of the
lover's malady. Her principal torment is of course the wound in her
breast—her passion for Scudamour—but Despight and Cruelty are add-
ing to her pain, for, like Britomart, she is constrained by decorum to
play the role of the "despitous" lady.[9]

Amoret's position in the line of march indicates the stage she has
reached in love's progress. The figures that follow her in the masque

---

[9] Roche believes that Despight and Cruelty are Amoret's principal tormentors
and that she "is being punished for her long resistance to the power of love"
(*Kindly Flame*, p. 75).

represent her future history if she remains Cupid's thrall. Reproach, Repentance, and Shame are inevitable and so are described in detail.

> And after them a rude confused rout
> Of persons flockt, whose names is hard to read:
> Emongst them was sterne Strife, and Anger stout,
> Unquiet Care, and fond Unthriftihead,
> Lewd Losse of Time, and Sorrow seeming dead,
> Inconstant Chaunge, and false Disloyaltie,
> Consuming Riotise, and guilty Dread
> Of heavenly vengeance, faint Infirmitie,
> Vile Povertie, and lastly Death with infamie.
>   (III.xii.25)

The mere service of Cupid cannot in Spenser's conception continue indefinitely. If passionate love is not soon transformed into temperate marital affection, if Amoret is not soon released from Busyrane's power, those figures waiting in the lady's vague future will become actual. But the conclusion of the masque is still doubtful; like the *Arcadia*, the drama may yet turn out to be a tragicomedy.

The only effective weapon against Busyrane is reason. It was not with the magic lance, emblem of her own passion for Artegall, that Britomart overcame the wall of fire. Still armed with reason and therefore undismayed by "idle shewes" and "false charmes," the lady knight has now reached Busyrane's ultimate stronghold, the inner chamber in which he and Amoret dwell surrounded by the masquers of Cupid. As Britomart enters, the masquers vanish.

> Ne living wight she saw in all that roome,
> Save that same woefull Ladie, both whose hands
> Were bounden fast, that did her ill become,

THE FAERIE QUEENE

And her small wast girt round with iron bands,
Unto a brasen pillour, by the which she stands.

And her before the vile Enchaunter sate,
Figuring straunge characters of his art,
With living bloud he those characters wrate,
Dreadfully dropping from her dying hart,
Seeming transfixed with a cruell dart,
And all perforce to make her him to love.
Ah who can love the worker of her smart?
A thousand charmes he formerly did prove;
Yet thousand charmes could not her stedfast heart remove.
                                              (III.xii.30–31)

Britomart compels the enchanter to lift his spells, and immediately
Amoret's wound is healed, the arrow drops from her heart, and she is
released from her chains. Departing with Amoret, the victorious champion is amazed to find no trace of the castle's "goodly roomes": the
chamber of gold, the hall of Cupid's wars, the fiery porch, just as in
Ariosto all the emblems of passion vanish at reason's triumph.

Amoret's prison disappears because it is unreal. Reality, truth, is the
world that reason perceives: the world in which the lover dwells is a
weird phantasmagoria sprung from his own diseased mind. Passion is
indeed a kind of enchanter, a perverter of the truth, suitably named
Busyrane to recall the old word "abusion" (deception). Busyrane's
name probably also alludes to the mythical tyrant Busiris, known for
making sacrifices of visitors to his kingdom.[10] The great danger for the
lover is that by becoming content with this enchanted world, by learning to relish passion for its own sake, he may become a sacrifice to

---

[10] The connection between Busyrane and abusion is pointed out by Roche,
pp. 82–83, who also discusses the allusion to Busiris. On Busiris, see Warton,
Var. III, 287, and Diodorus Siculus, *The Library of History*, IV.27.

125

Cupid. Busyrane, striving to win his prisoner's affection, desires her to do just that, to fall in love with love itself and become a willing worshiper before the blind god's image. But Amoret is not so deluded as to enjoy torment: she has no affection for "the worker of her smart" and therefore can be rescued from the enchanter's prison.

At one point in their struggle, Busyrane manages to wound Britomart with his knife:

> *Unwares it strooke into her snowie chest,*
> *That little drops empurpled her faire brest.*
> *Exceeding wroth therewith the virgin grew,*
> *Albe the wound were nothing deepe imprest,*
> *And fiercely forth her mortall blade she drew,*
> *To give him the reward for such vile outrage dew.*
> *(III.xii.33)*

The incident recalls Gardante's treachery at Castle Joyous, a blow described in terms strikingly similar, as well as the original wound received at her first sight of Artegall's image. Like Gardante, Busyrane represents an aspect of Cupid, and all three wounds refer to the same event, Britomart's induction into passionate love. It is for her own sake as well as Amoret's that Britomart battles Busyrane: she, too, is in danger of becoming a votary of Cupid, as Spenser indicates when he tells how difficult she found it to remove her eyes from the idol, "But ever more and more upon it gazed, / The whiles the passing brightnes her fraile sences dazed" (III.xi.49). Britomart's future is of course never in serious doubt, for Spenser always assures us that her injuries are light, by which he means that she never so completely yields to passion that her reason cannot reassert itself.

Unlike Britomart, Amoret has a definite allegorical signification. Each lover aspiring to the joy of marriage must free his Amoret, his own

126

loving soul, from the toils of the enchanter: to do this, to replace extreme passion with temperate affection, is to climb the final and most difficult rung on the ladder of married love. Sidney also understood this rung of the ladder. In the beautiful epithalamium sung by Dicus in the *Arcadia* he speaks of marriage as a state "Where justest love doth vanquish Cupid's powers / And warr of thoughts is swallow'd up in peace." In checking their youthful passions and marrying the princesses, Pyrocles and Musidorus too are freeing themselves from Busyrane's prison, vanquishing Cupid.

At the end of the *Arcadia* Sidney tells us of the children born to the noble couples and delicately suggests the nature of wedded joy. But in the original ending of Book III Spenser, describing Amoret and Scudamour's reunion, gives us more, a vivid image of the bliss to which the ladder of love ultimately leads.

> Lightly he clipt her twixt his armes twaine,
>   And streightly did embrace her body bright,
>   Her body, late the prison of sad paine,
>   Now the sweet lodge of love and deare delight:
>   But she faire Lady overcommen quight
>   Of huge affection, did in pleasure melt,
>   And in sweete ravishment pourd out her spright:
>   No word they spake, nor earthly thing they felt,
> But like two senceles stocks in long embracement dwelt.
>
> Had ye them seene, ye would have surely thought,
>   That they had beene that faire Hermaphrodite,
>   Which that rich Romane of white marble wrought,
>   And in his costly Bath causd to bee site:
>   So seemd those two, as growne together quite,
>   That Britomart halfe envying their blesse,
>   Was much empassiond in her gentle sprite,

HEROIC LOVE

And to her selfe oft wisht like happinesse,
In vaine she wisht, that fate n'ould let her yet possesse.
(III.xii.45–46, original version)

For Amoret and Scudamour, passion's sad pain has become the dear delight of wedded joy. The reconciliation of love and temperance prophesied by the encounter between Britomart and Guyon has been achieved. A man shall leave his father and mother and cleave unto his wife, says the Bible, and they shall be one flesh: and in Spenser's image of the hermaphrodite, ancient symbol of human perfection, Amoret and Scudamour are literally one flesh.[11] For Britomart, however, once again "empassiond in her gentle sprite," the end is not yet. Her marriage to Artegall, like Redcross' final union with his lady, is not to come, in all likelihood, until the grand conclusion of the epic at the feast of the Faerie Queene in Book XII—and that apocalyptic conclusion Spenser never lived to write.

THE HARMONY OF LOVE

When Spenser extended his epic in 1596, he revised the ending of Book III so that Amoret and Scudamour's adventures could continue in Book IV, the book of friendship. In this later version, the lovers' reunion and the simile of the hermaphrodite are omitted, Britomart and Amoret emerging from the enchanted castle to find that Scudamour has departed in despair. Book III deals primarily with the lover's problems before marriage. Book IV takes us beyond the wedding and considers

[11]Mark 10:7–8. See Lewis, *Allegory of Love*, p. 344; and Roche, pp. 133–136, who has found precedents for the hermaphrodite as a symbol of marriage in contemporary emblem books.

the problems Scudamour and Amoret must face after marriage. In the larger scheme of 1596, the final union of husband and wife cannot come until friendship has been added to love, that is, when harmony within wedlock has been achieved.

Book IV opens with a brief description of Amoret's wedding, thus glancing backward to Book III to place the Busyrane episode in clearer perspective, and also looking forward to new episodes by establishing that the lady is now a wife. Amoret's present task is to find Scudamour, or in other words to win her husband's trust and understanding. Spenser shows us Amoret and Britomart on their quest,

> Marching in lovely wise, that could deserve
> No spot of blame, though spite did oft assay
> To blot her with dishonor of so faire a pray.
> (IV.i.4)

This presentation of the travelers' relationship gracefully initiates the theme that dominates Amoret's story in Book IV, the honor and reputation of a married woman.

Amoret, who values honor more than life, assumes that Britomart is a man and fears for her good name. Although she need not distrust her companion, the lady's general concern is warranted, as we realize when the travelers arrive at a castle where Amoret is an object of widespread admiration. One "jolly knight" acts so boldly, in fact, that Britomart must take up arms to protect the young wife. This first assault is a preliminary to graver matters. Leaving the castle, the travelers encounter an unsavory quartet consisting of Duessa, Ate, Blandamour, and Paridell. Once again Amoret's beauty inspires a "jollie youthfull knight" to fond thoughts, this time the faithless Blandamour, who draws from Britomart the usual stout response. After the ladies' departure, however, Blandamour gets his revenge, for Scudamour appears and is deceived into believing that his wife is playing him false with her new champion. Bursting with wrath, Scudamour curses Britomart, and thus, at the end of the first canto, trust has yielded to suspicion and "wicked discord" has rent the fabric of marriage.

Scudamour's error is that, still inexperienced and unaware of the special loyalty marriage demands, he has judged his wife not as a loving husband should but according to the common fashion of the world, giving credence to the cruel voices of deceit. Just how poorly the world generally judges is shown at Satyrane's tournament, described in the fourth and fifth cantos, in which Venus' girdle is awarded to the false Florimell rather than to Amoret, the authentic embodiment of "chast love, / And wivehood true" (IV.v.3). Errors in Spenser do not go unpunished, and the result of Scudamour's distrust is that he finds himself in the House of Care, tormented by the violent workings of jealousy. This self-inflicted pain recalls the agony of Malbecco in Book III, where Spenser first suggested the destructiveness of jealousy in marriage. But Scudamour is not naturally mean-spirited and Amoret is no Hellenore. In the next episode the young husband discovers Britomart's sex and realizes his folly: henceforth he will not allow suspicion to poison the harmony of marriage.

Although Scudamour's faith has been restored, he is dismayed to find that his bride is no longer in Britomart's company. One day, Britomart explains,

> as through a desert wild
> We travelled, both wearie of the way
> We did alight, and sate in shadow mild;
> Where fearelesse I to sleepe me downe did lay.
> But when as I did out of sleepe abray,

130

THE FAERIE QUEENE

I found her not, where I her left whileare,
But thought she wandred was, or gone astray.
I cal'd her loud, I sought her farre and neare;
But no where could her find, nor tidings of her heare.
                                        (IV.vi.36)

When Spenser's characters become "wearie of the way" and relax their guard, we know that something bad is about to happen. Two easy victories over the presumptuous desires of jolly knights evidently induced in Britomart a foolish complacency, and she is caught napping at the moment of danger. Amoret too, as we learn in the seventh canto, has been complacent, fearlessly strolling through the woods without her companion, and as a result she has been seized by the monster Lust.

Amoret's imprisonment in the cave of Lust recalls the Busyrane episode but, whereas the enchanter represented a power within her soul, Lust is an external threat, the debased world, mounting its third and most frightening attack on her married honor. Lust is no gay trifler like the first bold knight, nor even a fickle ne'er-do-well like Blandamour: this is a thug, a common rapist, the "shame of men, and plague of womankind" (IV.vii.18). No longer a cloistered virgin, Amoret is learning the hard way about the perils of living in the world.[1]

---

[1] The history of Aemylia, Amoret's companion in captivity, suggests that Lust is not a representation of Amoret's own sexual desires, as has sometimes been assumed (as in Williams, *Spenser's "Faerie Queene,"* pp. 128–129). Passionately in love with Amyas, a young man socially unacceptable to her parents, Aemylia had arranged a tryst with her lover in a nearby grove, but on his way to the meeting the young man was overcome by Corflambo, who inspires lustful fire in his victims. Arriving at the grove, Aemylia found in her lover's place Lust, who carried her off to his cave. Plainly the monster here represents not Aemylia but Amyas himself, inflamed with desire. The story, related in the seventh and eighth cantos of Book IV, is a warning to young ladies of the dangers to which they may expose themselves by disobeying their parents and is analogous to Amoret's story, a warning of the dangers that lie in wait for the unwary wife.

HEROIC LOVE

Amoret's attempted escape from the cave fails and her plight seems worse than ever when Belphoebe and her servant Timias, representatives of the nobler elements of society, come to the rescue. Timias can only fend off the monster, but Belphoebe as a virgin is able to slay him: Spenser is perhaps suggesting the difference between the continent man, who can resist temptation, and the temperate man, who no longer even feels it. Belphoebe returns from slaying the monster to find Amoret unconscious in Timias' arms and so completely misjudges the situation that she departs in a huff. How Timias recovers his standing with Belphoebe need not concern us here; more important is that Amoret has been sorely wounded. Her injuries, received not only from Lust but also, inadvertently, from Timias, reflect the damage to her public reputation as a result of spending time with the monster and then being discovered in compromising circumstances with the squire. The wounds compel her, as we learn in the eighth canto, to take up a secluded existence in the woods. There, outcast from society as if in fact a fallen woman, she lives in pain until the day when Arthur, Spenser's magnanimous man, comes to heal her and guide her safely through the House of Sclaunder.

Amoret's recovery of her reputation, her emergence from the House of Sclaunder, is the natural climax of her adventures as a young wife. She has been introduced to the dangers that threaten a woman's honor and reputation, both in her husband's eyes and those of the world, and she is prepared now for reunion with Scudamour. But whether the couple is actually reunited in Book IV is uncertain because the text becomes confused. The problem arises at the end of the ninth canto when Arthur meets Scudamour, who complains to him about his lost lady. Presumably Amoret is still where Arthur has left her a short distance off, but the prince says nothing and the narrative passes on to the story of how Scudamour won his bride at the Temple of Venus. Possibly Spenser never intended the lovers to meet here, but in that

132

case the start of Scudamour's tale, in which he speaks of Amoret as if she were present, is extremely peculiar. According to Upton, they were to meet and Spenser planned to reintroduce here the image of the hermaphrodite from the original ending of Book III.[2] If Upton's suggestion is correct, as I believe it is, then Scudamour's tale of winning Amoret acquires significance as a grand conclusion to their adventures.

The story tells how the young knight proves his worth by forging past Doubt, Delay, and Danger, each falling away before his enchanted shield, the emblem of his love. The episode is an allegory of courtship after the fashion of the *Roman de la Rose*, but its significance is broader than that of the usual garden of love. Stationed on the temple porch, for example, is not the Cupid one might expect but a grander figure, Dame Concord, she by whom

> *the heaven is in his course contained,*
> *And all the world in state unmoved stands,*
> *As their Almightie maker first ordained.*
> *(IV.x.35)*

And the mysteriously veiled deity to whom Concord admits the knight is a Venus more awesome than the usual goddess of amatory verse. Hailed by her votaries with a hymn translated from the opening of Lucretius' *De rerum natura*, Spenser's goddess is Venus Genetrix, representative of all the creative powers of nature and of the love that binds individuals, families, nations, elements, planets, and stars in the vast harmony of the cosmos. In the presence of this awesome goddess the knight lays claim to his lady, stepping forward to take her hand. Amoret, educated in modesty and shamefastness, is naturally rather shy, but wedlock is her destiny and Venus is favoring this worthy knight's

---

[2] Scudamour speaks of Amoret as "she whom I behold" (IV.x.4). For Upton's suggestion, see *Var.* IV, 215–216.

boldness.[3] Thus Scudamour has won his Amoret, and thus Spenser has concluded his discussion of matrimony with a cosmic vision, revealing how the virtuous affection that binds man to woman in marriage is but one link in the fair chain of love that unites all things.

Chronologically, of course, this episode precedes Amoret's later history, both her captivity in the House of Busyrane and her experiences as a young wife. But Spenser has withheld it because not until now, after many trials, have Amoret and Scudamour really been united. By this time Scudamour knows love's pains well, but he has also discovered that such grace is given to lovers

> That all the cares and evill which they meet,
> May nought at all their setled mindes remove,
> But seeme gainst common sence to them most sweet;
> As bosting in their martyrdome unmeet.
> So all that ever yet I have endured,
> I count as naught, and tread downe under feete,
> Since of my love at length I rest assured,
> That to disloyalty she will not be allured.
>
> (IV.x.2)

Coming as it does at the end of Amoret and Scudamour's adventures, the story is a reaffirmation of love, an assurance that the pains and troubles lovers suffer are outweighed by the permanent joys of faithful union.

[3] In his description of the "tender teares" and "witching smiles" (IV.x.57) with which Amoret begs Scudamour to free her, Spenser probably intends no more than a charming picture of the reticence of a maiden who is taken from her familiar surroundings to enter upon a new and strange life. Perhaps too much has recently been made of Spenser's supposed psychological interest in Amoret's fear of sexual possession. See, for example, Nelson, *Poetry of Edmund Spenser,* pp. 230–231, 247–249, and Roche, *Kindly Flame,* pp. 72–88.

134

CONCLUSION

When the epic poets of the Renaissance decided to sing of love as well as war, a number of incidents from classical epic clung to their imaginations, and especially important were the stories of Circe and Odysseus and of Dido and Aeneas. In the Renaissance the story of the lady who seeks to divert the hero from his goal merged with the theme of the *Iliad*, the story of the great warrior Achilles, who rests idly in his tents as the Greek army fights its losing battles. This theme, that of the hero kept from war by the enchantments of a beautiful lady, appealed strongly to the half-medieval, half-classical taste of the sixteenth century.

For the sixteenth century the great hero, the hero par excellence, was not a character from epic but from mythology, Hercules. Dedicated to the pursuit of glory through arduous labors, Hercules was known as the conqueror of tyrants, the defender of political justice. He was also known as a moral hero, the prototype of the virtuous man who subdues his concupiscence. This, to us, rather surprising reputation was based upon a fable more familiar in the Renaissance than today, the story of how in his youth Hercules was presented with a choice between the ways of virtue and pleasure. Naturally he chose the steep and difficult path of virtue, and thus his glorious career began. Yet even this supreme hero once yielded to a beautiful lady. As the mythographer Natalis Comes put it, Hercules, "after having survived all dangers, after having quelled robbers and rid the earth of monsters, enslaved by his love for Omphale, committed base actions unworthy of his former deeds." [1] No doubt the story of Hercules' passion for Om-

---

[1] Quoted in C. W. Lemmi, "The Symbolism of the Classical Episodes in *The Faerie Queene*," *Philological Quarterly*, VIII (1929), 283–284. On Hercules, see Isabel E. Rathborne, *The Meaning of Spenser's Fairyland* (New York: Columbia University Press, 1937), pp. 89–104; Smith, *Elizabethan Poetry*, pp. 290–303; and Eugene M. Waith, *The Herculean Hero in Marlowe, Chapman, Shakespeare and Dryden* (New York: Columbia University Press, 1962), pp. 16–59.

CONCLUSION

phale—sometimes it is Iole he is said to have loved—contributed greatly to the appeal that the Greek hero held for the Renaissance. Certainly the image of him dressed in woman's clothes, reduced to the shame of the distaff and spinning wheel in punishment for his adventures of the heart, penetrated very deeply into the Renaissance imagination where, naturally enough, it became fused with Vergil's image of Aeneas' effeminacy at Dido's court.

We find the motif throughout the Renaissance epics. Ariosto's epic is organized around the paired characters of Orlando and Ruggiero, the greatest heroes respectively of the Christian and the Saracen armies. Orlando, in love with Angelica, has gone mad, and the forces of Charlemagne will not be victorious until he recovers his wits. The triumph of Christian over pagan will be complete when Ruggiero, the pagan champion, is baptized and married to Bradamante. But Ruggiero is hindered from fulfilling his destiny by his love for Alcina. Like Hercules, the proud Ruggiero has become effeminate, and Ariosto describes how the hero has changed his armor for necklaces, bracelets, and earrings, how he has perfumed and curled his hair until his appearance is altered beyond recognition.[2] After this, however, Ruggiero learns to control his concupiscence and eventually carries out his heroic destiny.

The pattern of the *Gerusalemme liberata* is similar. Once again victory over the infidel is delayed by the amorous exploits of the Christians' greatest hero. Jerusalem cannot be freed until Rinaldo has been extricated from the entanglements of Armida, who has carried him away to her palace of love in the Fortunate Isles. Carved upon the silver doors of Armida's palace is a portrait of Hercules tamely spinning amid Iole's maidens. The image suggests that Rinaldo has become another Hercules, although the hero himself does not realize this until messen-

[2] *Orlando furioso*, VII.54–55. In Harington's translation the passage comes at VII.46–47.

136

CONCLUSION

gers from the Christian army arrive and hold up a glittering shield in which he views his wanton, womanish attire.[3] After this shattering self-discovery, Rinaldo hastens back to the army and Jerusalem is at long last conquered.

The disfiguring passions of Pyrocles and Musidorus are obviously kin to the epic amours of their Italian cousins. Pyrocles is an Alcides in woman's clothes, and to remind himself of the Greek hero he has fastened his pretty gown with a jewel engraved with "a Hercules made in little fourme, but a distaffe set within his hand as he once was by Omphales commaundement" (I, 75–76). Artegall, the knight of justice, is also Hercules' man. For Spenser, the Greek hero is the prototype of all the great dispensers of justice, the hero who "all the West with equall conquest wonne, / And monstrous tyrants with his club sub-dewed." [4] But, like his prototype, Artegall finds himself enslaved by a woman, Radigund, and dressed in shameful clothes:

> Who had him seene, imagine mote thereby,
>   That whilome hath of Hercules bene told,
>   How for Iolas sake he did apply
>   His mightie hands, the distaffe vile to hold,
>   For his huge club, which had subdew'd of old
>   So many monsters, which the world annoyed;
>   His Lion's skin chaungd to a pall of gold,
>   In which forgetting warres, he onely joyed
> In combats of sweet love, and with his mistresse toyed.
>   (V.v.24)

[3] *Gerusalemme liberata*, XVI.30–31. For the carved image of Hercules, see XVI.3.

[4] V.i.2. On Hercules as the prototype of Artegall, see Rosemond Tuve, "Spenser's Reading: The *De Claris Mulieribus*," *Studies in Philology*, XXXIII (1936), 147–165.

CONCLUSION

The epic tradition tends to pit war against love, and to a certain extent the Elizabethan epics, especially the *Arcadia*, conform to this pattern. Pyrocles and Musidorus are diverted from their course of heroic action, seduced by the enchanting beauty of the Arcadian princesses. Like Ruggiero's and Rinaldo's experiences with passion, the princes' adventures in Arcadia are merely an interlude in lives otherwise devoted to heroic adventuring for the public good. Love has temporarily disguised them as the base shepherd and the effeminate warrior. But in order to return to the heroic life, Pyrocles and Musidorus do not disentangle themselves from their Omphales—rather they marry them. Love is not in fact a diversion from their true goal, but the final stage in their education, an experience arranged by providence to prepare them for their lives as rulers of states.

Spenser's treatment of the pattern emerging from the Italian epics is very similar to Sidney's.[5] Artegall is diverted from his life of public service by Radigund. She is his Alcina, and from her he must escape in order to wed his Bradamante. But, as we have seen, Radigund and Britomart are actually identical, the Amazon being a projection of Britomart as the cruel mistress from whom the knight must win mercy. Spenser's Hercules, too, is marrying his Omphale. For Spenser as well as Sidney, the experience of love is an education, a process of self-realization. We remember that Artegall before meeting Britomart was disguised as the Salvage Knight: in order to become his true self, the wise and gentle knight of Britomart's vision in the mirror, he has to

[5] Spenser, of course, employs the epic pattern not once but many times in *The Faerie Queene*, adapting it to purposes besides those used in his discussion of love. The pattern is clearly present in Book II, where Acrasia is the heir of nearly every temptress of the tradition. It also informs Book I, where to achieve his mission Redcross must disentangle himself from Duessa and return to the arms of Una.

be conquered by his lady. Love is no more a diversion for him than it is for Pyrocles and Musidorus.

If Radigund represents one aspect of the enchanting tyrant of tradition, another is embodied in Busyrane, possessed of the same magical powers that the epic poets assign to their Circes and Armidas. By witchcraft the great heroes are diverted from their virtuous courses and compelled to live in luxury and sloth. Like these heroes, Amoret is magically held in captivity, and her history repeats, at a high level of allegorical abstraction, their experiences in love, showing how love itself must be freed from the enchanter, passion. As we have seen, Amoret's history reflects Britomart's experiences: the lady knight, too, has been troubled by the enchanter and has found herself at odds with the virtuous knight of temperance. Although the central romance of the Ariostan part of *The Faerie Queene* thus displays the pattern of the hero kept from virtue by love, neither Britomart nor Artegall can justly be said to have been diverted from the proper goal, and Britomart can hardly be said to have yielded to sloth. For Britomart and Artegall, virtuous union with the beloved is itself a heroic goal, and passionate love is not so much a threat as it is a trial and a promise of the more virtuous state to follow.

Sidney and Spenser, then, do not really pit war against love in the fashion of the Italian poems. Instead they cast over love itself the atmosphere of the heroic, transforming the torments of the soul aspiring to marriage into a struggle worthy of the epic hero. To be struck by Cupid's arrow is still to fall from the virtuous state of temperance, but it is also, in the Protestant view, to receive a divine calling to marriage. To the commonsensical mind of England, the ladder of love leads to no heights of transcendent wisdom but to the placid virtues of sensible domesticity. Beneath the aristocratic rhetoric, beneath the fine heroics

CONCLUSION

of the *Arcadia* and *The Faerie Queene,* lurks the same homeliness that informs those Elizabethan dialogues in which the ideal figure is not the glamorous courtier but the perfect husband. Sidney and Spenser may have composed their poems in the grand tradition, but beneath the epic magnificence breathes the native spirit of Elizabethan England.

BIBLIOGRAPHY

INDEX

BIBLIOGRAPHY

Allen, Walter. *The English Novel: A Short Critical History*. London: Phoenix House Ltd., 1954.

Alpers, Paul J. *The Poetry of "The Faerie Queene."* Princeton: Princeton University Press, 1967.

Andrews, Mark Edwin. *Law versus Equity in "The Merchant of Venice."* Boulder: University of Colorado Press, 1965.

Ariosto, Ludovico. *Orlando furioso*, ed. Santorre Debenedetti and Cesare Segre. Bologna: Commissione per i Testi di Lingua, 1960.

—— *Orlando Furioso in English Heroical Verse*, trans. John Harington. London, 1591.

Atkinson, Dorothy F. "Busirane's Castle and Artidon's Cave," *Modern Language Quarterly*, I (1940), 185–192.

Babb, Lawrence. *The Elizabethan Malady: A Study of Melancholia in English Literature from 1580 to 1642*. East Lansing: Michigan State College Press, 1951.

Baker, Herschel. *The Dignity of Man: Studies in the Persistence of an Idea*. Cambridge: Harvard University Press, 1947.

Bembo, Pietro. *Gli Asolani*, trans. Rudolf B. Gottfried. Bloomington: Indiana University Press, 1954.

Bennett, Josephine Waters. *The Evolution of "The Faerie Queene."* Chicago: University of Chicago Press, 1942.

—— "Reply: On Methods of Literary Interpretation," *Journal of English and Germanic Philology*, XLI (1942), 486–489.

—— "Spenser's Garden of Adonis," *PMLA*, XLVII (1932), 46–80.

—— "Spenser's Garden of Adonis Revisited," *Journal of English and Germanic Philology*, XLI (1942), 53–78.

Bowers, Fredson. "Evidences of Revision in *The Faerie Queene* III.i,ii," *Modern Language Notes*, LX (1945), 114–116.

Bredvold, Louis I. "The Naturalism of Donne in Relation to Some Renaissance Traditions," *Journal of English and Germanic Philology*, XXII (1923), 471–502.

143

BIBLIOGRAPHY

Brooke, N. S. "C. S. Lewis and Spenser: Nature, Art and the Bower of Bliss," *The Cambridge Journal*, II (1949), 420–434.

Bruno, Giordano. *The Heroic Frenzies*, trans. Paul Eugene Memmo, Jr. Chapel Hill: University of North Carolina Press, 1965.

Burton, Robert. *The Anatomy of Melancholy*, ed. A. R. Shilleto. 3 vols. London: George Bell and Sons, 1896.

Bush, Douglas. *Mythology and the Renaissance Tradition in English Poetry*, rev. ed. New York: W. W. Norton and Co., 1963.

Calvin, John. *Institutes of the Christian Religion*, trans. John Allen, 7th ed. 2 vols. Philadelphia: Presbyterian Board of Christian Education, 1936.

Campbell, Lily B. *Shakespeare's Tragic Heroes: Slaves of Passion*. New York: Barnes and Noble, 1952.

Castiglione, Baldassare. *The Book of the Courtier*, trans. Sir Thomas Hoby, ed. Walter Raleigh. London: D. Nutt, 1900.

Challis, Lorna. "The Use of Oratory in Sidney's *Arcadia*," *Studies in Philology*, LXII (1965), 561–576.

Chaucer, Geoffrey. *The Works*, ed. F. N. Robinson, 2nd ed. Boston: Houghton Mifflin Co., 1957.

Cheney, Donald. *Spenser's Image of Nature: Wild Man and Shepherd in "The Faerie Queene."* New Haven: Yale University Press, 1966.

Cooper, Clyde Barnes. *Some Elizabethan Opinions of the Poetry and Character of Ovid*. Menasha, Wisc.: George Banta Publishing Co., 1914.

Crane, Thomas Frederick. *Italian Social Customs of the Sixteenth Century and Their Influence on the Literatures of Europe*. New Haven: Yale University Press, 1920.

Danby, John F. *Poets on Fortune's Hill: Studies in Sidney, Shakespeare, Beaumont and Fletcher*. London: Faber and Faber, 1952.

Davis, Walter R. "Actaeon in Arcadia," *Studies in English Literature*, II (1962), 95–110.

———— "A Map of Arcadia: Sidney's Romance in Its Tradition," in *Sidney's Arcadia*. New Haven and London: Yale University Press, 1965.

De Mornay, Philippe. *A Woorke Concerning the Trewnesse of the Christian Religion*, trans. Sir Philip Sidney and Arthur Golding. London, 1587.

Denomy, Alexander J. "Courtly Love and Courtliness," *Speculum*, XXVIII (1953), 44–63.

———— "*Fin' Amors*: The Pure Love of the Troubadours, Its Amorality, and Possible Source," *Mediaeval Studies*, VII (1945), 139–207.

144

BIBLIOGRAPHY

———— *The Heresy of Courtly Love.* New York: D. X. McMullen Co., 1947.

Dickey, Franklin M. *Not Wisely But Too Well: Shakespeare's Love Tragedies.* San Marino, Calif.: Huntington Library, 1957.

Duhamel, P. Albert. "Sidney's *Arcadia* and Elizabethan Rhetoric," *Studies in Philology*, XLV (1948), 134–150.

Duncan-Jones, Katherine D. "Sidney's Urania," *Review of English Studies*, XVII (1966), 123–132.

Einstein, Lewis. *The Italian Renaissance in England: Studies.* New York: Columbia University Press, 1913.

———— *Tudor Ideals.* New York: Harcourt, Brace and Co., 1921.

Ellrodt, Robert. *Neoplatonism in the Poetry of Spenser.* Geneva: Librairie E. Droz, 1960.

Ficino, Marsilio. *Commentary on Plato's Symposium,* trans. Sears Reynolds Jayne. Columbia: University of Missouri Press, 1944.

Fowler, Alastair. "Six Knights at Castle Joyous," *Studies in Philology*, LVI (1959), 583–599.

Galpin, Stanley Leman. *Cortois and Vilain: A Study of the Distinctions Made Between Them by the French and Provençal Poets of the 12th, 13th, and 14th Centuries.* New Haven: Ryder's Printing House, 1905.

George, Charles H. and Katherine. *The Protestant Mind of the English Reformation, 1570–1640.* Princeton: Princeton University Press, 1961.

Giamatti, A. Bartlett. *The Earthly Paradise and the Renaissance Epic.* Princeton: Princeton University Press, 1966.

Gilbert, Allan H. "The Ladder of Lechery, *The Faerie Queene*, III.i.45," *Modern Language Notes*, LVI (1941), 594–597.

———— ed. *Literary Criticism: Plato to Dryden.* New York: American Book Co., 1940.

Godshalk, William Leigh. "Sidney's Revision of the *Arcadia*, Books III–V," *Philological Quarterly*, XLIII (1964), 171–184.

Golding, Arthur. *Shakespeare's Ovid: Being Arthur Golding's Translation of the Metamorphoses,* ed. W. H. D. Rouse. London: Centaur Press, 1961.

Greene, Robert. *Morando: The Tritameron of Love.* London, 1584.

Greenlaw, Edwin. "Britomart at the House of Busirane," *Studies in Philology*, XXVI (1929), 117–130.

145

BIBLIOGRAPHY

———— "The Captivity Episode in Sidney's *Arcadia*," in *The Manly Anniversary Studies in Language and Literature*. Chicago: University of Chicago Press, 1923.

———— "Sidney's *Arcadia* as an Example of Elizabethan Allegory," in *Kittredge Anniversary Papers*. Boston and London: Ginn and Co., 1913.

Guth, Hans P. "Allegorical Implications of Artifice in Spenser's *Faerie Queene*," *PMLA*, LXXVI (1961), 474–479.

Haller, William. "Hail Wedded Love," *ELH*, XIII (1946), 79–97.

———— and Malleville Haller. "The Puritan Art of Love," *Huntington Library Quarterly*, V (1942), 235–272.

Hamilton, A. C. *The Structure of Allegory in "The Faerie Queene."* Oxford: Oxford University Press, 1961.

Hankins, John E. "The Sources of Spenser's Britomartis," *Modern Language Notes*, LVIII (1943), 607–610.

Harrison, John Smith. *Platonism in English Poetry of the Sixteenth and Seventeenth Centuries*. New York: Columbia University Press, 1903.

Harrison, T. P., Jr. "The Relations of Spenser and Sidney," *PMLA*, XLV (1930), 712–731.

Harrison, William. "The Description of England," in *Holinshed's Chronicles*. 6 vols. London, 1807–1808.

Hooker, Richard. *The Works*, ed. John Keble. 3 vols. Oxford: Oxford University Press, 1845.

Hoopes, Robert. *Right Reason in the English Renaissance*. Cambridge: Harvard University Press, 1962.

Hough, Graham. *A Preface to "The Faerie Queene."* London: Gerald Duckworth and Co., 1962.

Howard, George Elliott. *A History of Matrimonial Institutions Chiefly in England and the United States*. 3 vols. Chicago: University of Chicago Press, 1904.

Hutton, James. "Spenser and the 'Cinq Points en Amours,'" *Modern Language Notes*, LVII (1942), 657–661.

Isler, Alan D. "Heroic Poetry and Sidney's Two *Arcadias*," *PMLA*, LXXXIII (1968), 368–379.

Izard, Thomas C. *George Whetstone: Mid-Elizabethan Gentleman of Letters*. New York: Columbia University Press, 1942.

Jayne, Sears Reynolds. "Ficino and the Platonism of the English Renaissance," *Comparative Literature*, IV (1952), 214–238.

BIBLIOGRAPHY

John, Lisle Cecil. *The Elizabethan Sonnet Sequences: Studies in Conventional Conceits.* New York: Columbia University Press, 1938.

Jones, H. S. V. *A Spenser Handbook.* New York: Appleton-Century-Crofts, 1930.

Jordan, John Clark. *Robert Greene.* New York: Columbia University Press, 1915.

Kalstone, David. *Sidney's Poetry: Contexts and Interpretations.* Cambridge: Harvard University Press, 1965.

Kelso, Ruth. *The Doctrine of the English Gentleman in the Sixteenth Century.* Urbana: University of Illinois Press, 1929.

Kittredge, G. L. "Chaucer's Discussion of Marriage," *Modern Philology,* IX (1912), 435–467.

Kristeller, Paul Oskar. *The Philosophy of Marsilio Ficino,* trans. Virginia Conant. New York: Columbia University Press, 1943.

Lanham, Richard A. "The *Old Arcadia,*" in *Sidney's Arcadia.* New Haven and London: Yale University Press, 1965.

Lemmi, Charles W. "Britomart: The Embodiment of True Love," *Studies in Philology,* XXXI (1934), 133–139.

——— "The Symbolism of the Classical Episodes in *The Faerie Queene,*" *Philological Quarterly,* VIII (1929), 270–287.

Levinson, Ronald B. "The 'Godlesse Minde' in Sidney's *Arcadia,*" *Modern Philology,* XXIX (1931), 21–26.

Lewis, C. S. *The Allegory of Love: A Study in Medieval Tradition.* Oxford: Oxford University Press, 1936.

——— *English Literature in the Sixteenth Century Excluding Drama.* Oxford: Oxford University Press, 1954.

——— Review of Robert Ellrodt, *Neoplatonism in the Poetry of Spenser* (Geneva, 1960), in *Etudes anglaises,* XIV (1961), 107–116.

——— *Spenser's Images of Life,* ed. Alastair Fowler. Cambridge: Cambridge University Press, 1967.

Lindheim, Nancy Rothwax. "Sidney's *Arcadia,* Book II: Retrospective Narrative," *Studies in Philology,* LXIV (1967), 159–186.

Lipsius, Justus. *Two Bookes of Constancie,* trans. Sir John Stradling, ed. Rudolph Kirk and Clayton Morris Hall. New Brunswick: Rutgers University Press, 1939.

Lowes, J. L. "The Loveres Maladye of Hereos," *Modern Philology,* XI (1914), 491–546.

147

BIBLIOGRAPHY

MacLure, Millar. "Nature and Art in *The Faerie Queene,*" *ELH,* XXVIII (1961), 1–20.

Marlowe, Christopher. *The Works,* ed. C. F. Tucker Brooke. Oxford: Oxford University Press, 1910.

Mason, John E. *Gentlefolk in the Making: Studies in the History of English Courtesy Literature and Related Topics from 1531 to 1774.* Philadelphia: University of Pennsylvania Press, 1935.

McClennen, Joshua. *On the Meaning and Function of Allegory in the English Renaissance.* University of Michigan Contributions in Modern Philology, No. 6. Ann Arbor, 1947.

McMurphy, Susannah Jane. *Spenser's Use of Ariosto for Allegory.* University of Washington Publications in Language and Literature, II. Seattle, 1924.

Merrill, Robert Valentine. "Platonism in Petrarch's Canzoniere," *Modern Philology,* XXVII (1929), 161–174.

Milton, John. *Complete Prose Works,* ed. Don M. Wolfe et al. 4 vols. to date. New Haven: Yale University Press, 1953–.

——— *The Poetical Works,* ed. Helen Darbishire. 2 vols. Oxford: Oxford University Press, 1952.

Murray, Gilbert. *The Stoic Philosophy.* New York and London: G. P. Putnam's Sons, 1915.

Myrick, Kenneth O. *Sir Philip Sidney as a Literary Craftsman.* Cambridge: Harvard University Press, 1935.

Nelson, John Charles. *Renaissance Theory of Love: The Context of Giordano Bruno's Eroici Furori.* New York: Columbia University Press, 1958.

Nelson, William. *The Poetry of Edmund Spenser: A Study.* New York: Columbia University Press, 1963.

Overbury, Sir Thomas, et al. *The Overburian Characters to Which Is Added A Wife,* ed. W. J. Paylor. Oxford: Blackwell, 1936.

Owen, W. J. B. "The Structure of *The Faerie Queene,*" *PMLA,* LXVIII (1953), 1079–1100.

Painter, Sidney. *French Chivalry: Chivalric Ideas and Practices in Mediaeval France.* Baltimore: Johns Hopkins Press, 1940.

Parker, Pauline. *The Allegory of "The Faerie Queene."* Oxford: Oxford University Press, 1960.

Pearson, Lu Emily. *Elizabethan Love Conventions.* Berkeley: University of California Press, 1933.

BIBLIOGRAPHY

Petrarch, Francesco. *Il Canzoniere,* ed. Michele Scherillo, 3rd ed. Milan: U. Hoepli, 1918.

Powell, Chilton Latham. *English Domestic Relations 1487–1653: A Study of Matrimony and Family Life in Theory and Practice as Revealed by the Literature, Law, and History of the Period.* New York: Columbia University Press, 1917.

Puttenham, George. *The Arte of English Poesie,* ed. Gladys Doidge Willcock and Alice Walker. Cambridge: Cambridge University Press, 1936.

Rathborne, Isabel E. *The Meaning of Spenser's Fairyland.* New York: Columbia University Press, 1937.

Rees, Joan. "Fulke Greville and the Revisions of *Arcadia,*" *Review of English Studies,* XVII (1966), 54–57.

Robb, Nesca A. *Neoplatonism of the Italian Renaissance.* London: G. Allen and Unwin, 1935.

Roche, Thomas P., Jr. *The Kindly Flame: A Study of the Third and Fourth Books of Spenser's Faerie Queene.* Princeton: Princeton University Press, 1964.

Rose, Mark. "Sidney's Womanish Man," *Review of English Studies,* XV (1964), 353–363.

Rowe, Kenneth Thorpe. "Elizabethan Morality and the Folio Revisions of Sidney's *Arcadia,*" *Modern Philology,* XXXVII (1939), 151–172.

——— *Romantic Love and Parental Authority in Sydney's Arcadia.* University of Michigan Contributions in Modern Philology, No. 4. Ann Arbor, 1947.

Rudenstine, Neil L. *Sidney's Poetic Development.* Cambridge: Harvard University Press, 1967.

Scaglione, Aldo D. *Nature and Love in the Late Middle Ages.* Berkeley: University of California Press, 1963.

Shakespeare, William. *The Complete Works,* ed. Peter Alexander. London and Glasgow: Collins, 1951.

Sidney, Sir Philip. *The Poems,* ed. William A. Ringler, Jr. Oxford: Clarendon Press, 1962.

——— *The Prose Works,* ed. Albert Feuillerat. 4 vols. Cambridge: Cambridge University Press, 1962.

Smith, G. Gregory, ed. *Elizabethan Critical Essays.* 2 vols. Oxford: Oxford University Press, 1904.

Smith, Hallett. *Elizabethan Poetry: A Study in Conventions, Meaning, and Expression.* Cambridge: Harvard University Press, 1964.

BIBLIOGRAPHY

Spenser, Edmund. *The Works: A Variorum Edition,* ed. Edwin Greenlaw et al. 9 vols. Baltimore: Johns Hopkins Press, 1932–1949.

Spingarn, J. E. *A History of Literary Criticism in the Renaissance,* 2nd ed. New York and London: Columbia University Press, 1963.

Stevenson, David Lloyd. *The Love-Game Comedy.* New York: Columbia University Press, 1946.

St. German, Christopher. *Dialoges in Englishe, Betwixte a Doctoure of Divinitie, and a Student in the Laws of England.* London, 1569.

Stirling, Brents. "The Philosophy of Spenser's Garden of Adonis," *PMLA,* XLIX (1934), 501–538.

———— "Spenser's 'Platonic' Garden," *Journal of English and Germanic Philology,* XLI (1942), 482–486.

Syford, Constance Miriam. "The Direct Source of the Pamela-Cecropia Episode in the *Arcadia,*" *PMLA,* XLIX (1934), 472–489.

Tasso, Torquato. *Godfrey of Bulloigne, or The Recoverie of Jerusalem,* trans. Edward Fairfax. London, 1600.

———— *Poesie,* ed. Francesco Flora. Milan: Rizzoli, 1952.

Tatham, Edward H. R. *Francesco Petrarca: The First Modern Man of Letters.* 2 vols. London: Sheldon Press, 1925–1926.

Tillyard, E. M. W. *The English Epic and Its Background.* London: Chatto and Windus, 1954.

Tilney, Edmund. *A Brief and Pleasant Discourse of Duties in Marriage, Called The Flower of Friendshippe.* London, 1568.

Townsend, Freda L. "Sidney and Ariosto," *PMLA,* LXI (1946), 97–108.

Tuve, Rosemond. "Spenser's Reading: The De Claris Mulieribus," *Studies in Philology,* XXXIII (1936), 147–165.

Valency, Maurice. *In Praise of Love: An Introduction to the Love-Poetry of the Renaissance.* New York: Macmillan Co., 1958.

Vives, Lodovicus. *The Instruction of a Christen Woman,* trans. Richarde Hyrde. London, 1557.

Waith, Eugene M. *The Herculean Hero in Marlowe, Chapman, Shakespeare and Dryden.* New York: Columbia University Press, 1962.

Walker, D. P. "Ways of Dealing with Atheists: A Background to Pamela's Refutation of Cecropia," *Bibliothèque d'Humanisme et Renaissance,* XVII (1955), 252–277.

Watson, Foster. *Vives and the Renascence Education of Women.* New York: Longmans, Green and Co., 1912.

Whately, William. *A Bride-Bush.* London, 1619.

BIBLIOGRAPHY

Whetstone, George. *An Heptameron of Civill Discourses.* London, 1582.
Whitaker, Virgil K. *The Religious Basis of Spenser's Thought.* Stanford: Stanford University Press, 1950.
Whitney, Lois. "Concerning Nature in *The Countesse of Pembrokes Arcadia*," *Studies in Philology*, XXIV (1927), 207–222.
Williams, Kathleen. *Spenser's "Faerie Queene": The World of Glass.* London: Routledge and Kegan Paul, 1966.
Williams, Ralph Coplestone. "The Purpose of Poetry, and Particularly the Epic, as Discussed by Critical Writers of the Sixteenth Century in Italy," *Romanic Review*, XII (1921), 1–20.
Wolff, Samuel Lee. *The Greek Romances in Elizabethan Prose Fiction.* New York: Columbia University Press, 1912.
Woodhouse, A. S. P. "Nature and Grace in *The Faerie Queene*," *ELH*, XVI (1949), 194–228.
Wright, Celeste Turner. "The Amazons in Elizabethan Literature," *Studies in Philology*, XXXVII (1940), 433–456.
Wright, Louis B. *Middle-Class Culture in Elizabethan England.* Ithaca: Cornell University Press, 1963.
Wyatt, Sir Thomas. *Collected Poems,* ed. Kenneth Muir. Cambridge: Harvard University Press, 1950.
Wyclif, John. *Select English Works,* ed. Thomas Arnold. 3 vols. Oxford: Oxford University Press, 1869–1871.
Zandvoort, R. W. *Sidney's Arcadia: A Comparison Between the Two Versions.* Amsterdam, N. V. Swets and Zeitlinger, 1929.

INDEX

Achilles, 135
Achilles Tatius, 1, 37
Acrasia, 138n
Adonis, 87–88
Adonis, Garden of, 99, 118–121
Aemylia, 131n
Aeneas, 135–136
Allegory, 14, 81–82, 112–113
Amadis de Gaul, 37
Amazon, 50–52, 56. *See also* Radigund
Amoret, 110–111, 113–134, 139
Amphialus, 39, 61
Amyas, 131n
Anachronism, 58
Andreas Capellanus, 16
Andromana, 53
Antifeminism, 7–9, 38–39, 105
Antiphilus, 53
Apollo, 40, 56, 58, 63
Araignment of Lewd, Idle, Froward, and Unconstant Women, 8
Archimago, 80
Argalus and Parthenia, 39, 48, 66
Ariosto, Ludovico, 1, 2, 3, 77–79, 81, 93–94, 96–97, 112–113, 114, 125, 136, 138–139
Artegall, 77–79, 85, 88, 92–93, 98, 99, 100, 103–109, 110, 112, 124, 126, 137–139
Arthur, 83, 85, 132
Asceticism, 7–9, 20, 23, 27
Ate, 129

Basilius, 40, 42, 43, 49, 54, 55, 58, 62–63, 64, 67–68, 70–73

Belphoebe, 111, 132
Bembo, Pietro, 3, 19–22, 25, 26, 89
Bible, 128
Blandamour, 129–130, 131
Boccaccio, 13, 24
Bower of Bliss, 87
Bradamante. *See* Ariosto
Britomart: as chastity, 80–84, 109, 111; meets Guyon, 80–84; her spear, 82, 83, 105, 124; at Castle Joyous, 85–92; falls in love, 93–96; with Merlin, 96–100; meets Marinell, 100–102; meets Artegall, 103–105; frees Artegall from Radigund, 107–109; frees Amoret from Busyrane, 113–128; as Amoret's companion, 129–131; mentioned, 77–79, 110, 112, 139
Bruno, Giordano, 3, 19, 20–21
Burton, Robert, 9–10, 12
Busiris, 125
Busyrane, 109–128, 129, 134

Calvin, John, 14, 27, 111
Care, House of, 130
Castiglione, Baldassare, 3, 12, 19–22, 25–26
Castle Joyous, 79, 85–93, 100, 110, 115, 117, 121, 126
Cavalcanti, Guido, 16
Cecropia, 39, 60–65, 71
Chapman, George, 15–16
Charles I, 56–57
Chaucer, Geoffrey, 16–17, 23, 30–31, 110

153

INDEX

INDEX

Lucifera, 92
Lucretius, 23, 133
Lust, 48, 54–56, 62–63, 66, 87, 110, 115–116, 118, 121; character in *Faerie Queene*, 131–132
Luther, Martin, 111
Lyly, John, 3, 38

Malbecco, 102, 130
Malecasta, 79, 86–93, 100, 103, 109, 110, 113, 117
Malecasta, House of. *See* Castle Joyous
Malory, Sir Thomas, 37
Marinell, 80, 101–102, 110
Marlowe, Christopher, 14–15
Marriage, 3, 17–18, 24–26, 138–140; new dignity of, 26–29; romanticizing of, 30–34; in *Arcadia*, 55–56, 70–73; in *Faerie Queene*, 77–79, 80, 84, 98–99, 108, 109–113, 117–118, 121, 124, 126–134
Melissa, 79
Merlin, 79, 80, 96–100, 101, 103, 117
Meun, Jean de, 15
Milton, John, 28–29, 31, 32n, 56–57
Mirror for Magistrates, 8
Montemayor, Jorge de, 37
More, Sir Thomas, 29
Mornay, Philippe de, 14, 59n
Musidorus: in *Old Arcadia*, 37–41; reacts to Arcadia, 47–49; falls in love, 50; as Stoic, 59–60; imprisoned and tried, 68–73; mentioned, 43, 46, 51, 53, 55, 56, 57, 62, 64, 67, 127, 137–139

Nashe, Thomas, 11
Natalis Comes, 135
Nature, 60–63, 106, 133–134; vs. art, 119–121
Neoplatonism, 17, 18–24, 26, 34, 53, 111n, 118n, 119

Odysseus, 135
Old Arcadia, 37–41
Omphale, 135–136, 138
Overbury, Sir Thomas, 11
Ovid, 10, 14–15, 77, 94–95
Owl and the Nightingale, 17

Padelford, Frederick M., 80
Pamela, 38, 40, 41, 50, 53, 55, 63, 64–65, 67, 70–73, 138; religious beliefs and debate with Cecropia, 56–62
Pan, 56, 58
Paridell, 113, 129
Pastoral, 8, 41–43
Pégulhan, Aimeric de, 13
Pembroke, Countess of, 39–41
Perkins, William, 28
Petrarch, Francesco, 3, 18–19, 77
Petrarchism, 7, 22–23, 24, 101, 108–109, 121–122
Phalantus, 39
Philanax, 40, 49, 69, 71
Philoclea, 38, 40, 41, 46–47, 51–55, 58, 64–67, 70–73, 138
Plato, 23
Platonism. *See* Neoplatonism
Proteus, 110
Providence, 60, 64, 68, 72–73, 99–100
Puttenham, George, 9
Pyrocles: in *Old Arcadia*, 37–41; falls in love, 45–50; as Amazon, 50–51, 56; at cave, 54–55; considers suicide, 64–67; imprisoned and tried, 68–73; mentioned, 43, 52, 53, 57, 59, 63, 127, 137–139

Querelle des femmes, 7, 8

Radigund, 77, 106–108, 137–138
Raleigh, Sir Walter. *See* Spenser, letter to Raleigh.
Redcross Knight, 65, 77, 80, 81, 86n, 92, 128, 138n

155

INDEX